Promoting Positive Behaviors After School

Paul G. Young, Ph.D.

CreateSpace, An Amazon.com Company
Columbia, South Carolina
Available from Amazon.com and other retail outlets

ISBN: 9781793141514

Printed in the United States of America

Dedicated to afterschool program leaders and their staffs who artistically manage students each day with care, compassion, and commitment.

CONTENTS

Acknowledgments		viii
Introduction		1
Part 1	**Beginnings/Transitions** *Ideas and Advice That Support and Facilitate Smooth School-to-Afterschool Transitions, Efficacy of Time, and Effective Student Supervision*	11
1.1	Teach and Clarify the Program Mission and Vision	12
1.2	Define Discipline and Punishment	14
1.3	Develop a Code of Conduct	15
1.4	Build Relationships	17
1.5	Develop a Staff and Student Handbook	21
1.6	Structure Effective Meetings	22
1.7	The Staff Huddle	24
1.8	Plan for Effective Play Area Supervision During School-to-Afterschool	26
1.9	Involve Students and Volunteers with Transition Supervision	28
1.10	Teach Students How to Form Lines	28
1.11	Communicate Plans & Build Relationships with Parents	29
1.12	Teach Children to Move Quietly Through Hallways	32
1.13	Secure Your Program Area	33
1.14	Teach Etiquette & Dress Codes	33
1.15	Greet Students by Name and Look Them in the Eye	34
1.16	Check Mail and Messages At Least Twice Daily	34
	Checklist # 1 - Beginnings/Transitions—Structural Analysis and Assessment	37
Part 2	**Instruction and Learning** *Ideas and Advice That Enhance Instruction and Increase Student Achievement*	41
2.1	Supervise Student Transitions to and from Special Classes	42
2.2	Establish Procedures for Restroom Breaks	44
2.3	Practice Entering and Leaving Assemblies	45
2.4	Assure That Substitutes Have Adequate Plans	47
2.5	Time-on-Task	48

2.6	Establish Protocols for Referring Students to the Site-Director	48
2.7	Fully Utilize Volunteer Services	50
2.8	Schedule and Compensate Staff for Adequate Planning Time	50
	Checklist # 2 - Instruction and Learning—Structural Analysis and Assessment	53
Part 3	**Midpoints/Break Time/Meals & Snacks** *Ideas and Advice That Provide Students with Structure and Positive Behaviors When Needed Most*	57
3.1	Equip Staff for Mid-Program Supervisory Environments	58
3.2	Teach Manners & Personal Hygiene	60
3.3	Facilitate Efficient Food Serving Processes	60
3.4	Consider Play Time First, Eating Afterwards	61
3.5	Teach Children to Speak with Inside Voices	62
3.6	Structure Playground Games	63
3.7	Teach Adults How to Prevent Bullying	66
3.8	Establish Procedures for Indoor Play Activities	69
3.9	Take Pictures and Use Recorders	70
3.10	Establish Contingency Plans for Crisis Supervision	70
3.11	Teach Children to Speak in Complete Sentences	71
3.12	Help Children Gain the Verbal Advantage	72
3.13	Invite Guests to Observe	75
3.14	Develop a Conflict Mediation Program	79
3.15	Share Success with the School Principal	80
	Twenty Minute Meeting Agenda	81
	Checklist # 3 - Midpoints/Break Time/Meals & Snacks—Structural Analysis and Assessment	83
Part 4	**Second Half (After 5:00 p.m.)** *Ideas and Advice That Provide Positive Outcomes for Learners of All Ages*	87
4.1	Reading Is Always a Positive Learning Activity	88
4.2	Write Personal Notes and Make Positive Phone Calls	89
4.3	Teach Multiple Intelligences	90
4.4	Teach the Concepts of Grit and Mindset	92
4.5	Understand How Trauma and Toxic Stress Impacts Behavior	96
4.6	Create an "Adam Plan"	97
4.7	Encourage Children to Draw	100
4.8	Provide Staff with Support	100
4.9	Solve the Homework Conundrums	101
4.10	Create a "Purple Cow" Effect for Your Program	103
	Checklist # 4 - Second Half (After 5:00 p.m.) Structural Analysis and Assessment	107

Part 5	**Endings (Dismissal Time and Wrap-Up of the Year)** *Ideas, Advice, and Reflections that Reinforce Positive Behaviors When Things Wind Down*	111
5.1	Establish a Positive Pick-up Environment and Process	113
5.2	Ride School Buses	114
5.3	Walk Students Home	114
5.4	Establish Curb Appeal	115
5.5	Eliminate Gum	115
5.6	Alert Bosses About Potential Problems	116
5.7	Be a Master Motivator	116
5.8	Toot Your Own Horn	118
5.9	Align the School and Afterschool Program Learning Opportunities	118
	Checklist # 5 - Endings **Structural Analysis and Assessment**	123
	Rubric Explanation of the Structural Analysis and Assessment Levels	126
	The Five Stages of Afterschool Instructional Mastery	128
Appendices		
1	The Afterschool Program Culture Survey	129
2	ACEs Survey	130
3	50 Positive Comments to Make with Children and Youth	131
4	In this afterschool program, it is "cool" to…	132
5	Responsibility Checklist for the Principal and After-School Program Director	133
6	Common Non-Verbal Communication Techniques	135
7	Educational Acronyms	136
Index		137
Other Books by Paul G. Young		140
About the Author		143
References and Recommended Reading		145

ACKNOWLEDGMENTS

My venture into the world of after school education has been two-fold. My first job in the 70s-80s was as a high school band director which required many hours of practice after the school day for various ensembles, especially marching band. As I reflect, those times working with young musicians beyond the school day proved to be a wonderful afterschool program, even though we never called it that. Now, research findings affirm that participation in extracurricular activities enables students to develop what developmental psychologists call *soft* skills, traits that are difficult to attain yet crucial for success. My students learned many music and performance competencies, but just as importantly they gained skills of self-discipline, grit, creativity, collaboration, growth mindset, and critical thinking.

Decades later, while serving in my final elementary school principalship, I was fortunate to play a key role in the development of an afterschool program created to provide needy students extra time to learn – after school – to complete homework, remediate and develop skills, and be provided with care and attention in a safe, nurturing environment. What started as a community volunteer program grew and developed into a 501(c)(3), model 21st Century Community Learning Center (21st CCLC) that continues to serve my former school community and other elementary and middle schools throughout the school district.

It is to all the hard working, dedicated individuals I've been fortunate to meet and work with through various local, state, and national professional networks that I am grateful for the leadership lessons they shared with me. These individuals are too numerous to mention or list here, but collectively they shared a common philosophy – *pay it forward.* That is my intention with this book. I hope emerging afterschool leaders will find the tips, insights, and advice contained within to be as helpful to them as I did when they were introduced to me.

The people associated with the afterschool programs in my hometown of Lancaster, Ohio – past, present, and future – will always hold a special place in my heart. I have tremendous appreciation for the ongoing support of my wife, Gertrude, and our daughters and sons-in-law, Katie and Jon Steele, and Mary Ellen and Eric Rahn, especially for their encouragement to write, train, and consult in a field that is very special to me. I hope my influence will, in turn, benefit professionals in afterschool programs who will someday care for my grandchildren, Nora and Evan Rahn, and Charlie and "Jack" (Jonathan Paul) Steele.

Paul G. Young
Lancaster, Ohio,
January 2019

Introduction

Afterschool = hard work! Reading this, if you work in the afterschool field in almost any type of position, you know firsthand all that that statement involves. Yet even though the work is hard, it is generally fun and rewarding, especially when the students enrolled in the program are displaying their best behavior. But as anyone who has ever worked with kids knows, they do not always behave in positive ways. If you've chosen to read this book, there is a good likelihood that the title caught your attention and you are searching for tips and strategies that will help improve your students' behavior. My goal is to provide advice, tools, and insights from lessons learned that will empower you to structure a learning environment so that positive behaviors (of both adults and students) become the norm.

More than 45 years ago, I started my first job as a high school band director. One of my responsibilities was to lead and direct the marching band – a very important program and source of pride for the community. As a co-curricular offering, the band met the last period of the day (for which students earned a grade and credit) but rehearsals also extended into the hours after school. Even though my first "after school" program might have been somewhat different than yours, I still faced the challenges of any young educator – in school or after school. Mostly, I wanted the kids to be good and do what I told them to do when I told them to do it.

I found myself facing a steep learning curve, along with my assistant director (also new). We were in charge of nearly 150 musicians in grades 9-12. They had a great tradition of excellence. Now, pressure mounted to maintain and sustain those good patterns of disciplined performance. I can no longer recall the degree of intimidation or fear I must have experienced, but I do remember feeling very vulnerable when I was unprepared or failed to make my expectations clear. Even now, while working with college students, my lack of preparation of clarity usually results in their less-than-positive performance. It would be easy to blame them for poor attitudes, inattentiveness, and lack of motivation, but I've learned they can't know and react positively in ways that I want them to *if I don't tell them.*

Later, as a 20-year veteran principal, I was fortunate to serve in leadership roles with the Ohio Association of Elementary School Administrators (OAESA), the National Association of Elementary School Principals (NAESP), and the National AfterSchool Association (NAA). I realized my trials and tribulations with student management and behavior were being experienced everywhere in the nation. Not every leader, however, was able to understand how attention to the little things contribute to an overall school or afterschool program structure of success. Even alone in my college classrooms, the structures that I effectively established, or those that I failed to create, greatly impacted and determined the degree of success and satisfaction my students and I experienced.

I was assigned to be the principal of West School in Lancaster, Ohio, in August 1996. The school was located in one of the city's poorest precincts in the shadow of the main manufacturing plant for Anchor Hocking Glassware. Like many midwestern manufacturing towns, Anchor Hocking, originally locally-owned, had been sold on Wall Street. As a result, Lancaster steadily had experienced the loss of the company executives and a significant portion of its prosperity. The West School neighborhood reflected the decline – decaying homes owned and rented to non-working parents by phantom landlords, homelessness, drugs, increased crime, transience, etc. West School had acquired a reputation as a tough school. The kids and their parents brought many of their challenges to school. At first, my office was often full of students referred for my intervention. I quickly realized we needed better structure and a common vision of how our school would function.

The contents of this book mirror the results of the hours of self-and-group reflection of my staffs during a nine-year year tenure at the school. Amidst much hard work, together, West School was transformed from a school of significant negativity with high numbers of detentions, school and after-school suspensions, fights, and theft into a calm, orderly atmosphere where sometimes weeks would go by without a serious office referral. Some might describe the strategies described in this book as old school; I prefer to acknowledge them as tips taught to me by master teachers and administrators that have withstood the test of time and work anywhere and anytime when adults do what they should know and be able to do.

In January 2005, after retiring from the principalship, I became the Executive Director of the West After School Center, a program which I had helped start while serving as the West School principal. The program aided kids from my school and was housed in a newly-built facility directly across the street from the school's playground. To create a positive culture, I implemented the behavioral and structural strategies that had worked for the school. I had also witnessed them successfully replicated in other schools by my young principal mentees. Good structure is the key element of success, anywhere.

In 2008, with publishing assistance from Corwin Press and NAESP, I wrote *Promoting Positive Behaviors: An Elementary Principal's Guide to Structuring the Learning Environment*. This endeavor was my way of giving back to my principal colleagues who taught me how to organize, structure, and lead a school so that students and staff would perform in positive ways. Even though school and afterschool programs across the nation vary and have unique needs, there are common complexities within times of the day and year that can be analyzed and addressed using shared structures. It became a popular handbook among principals. Later, while working for NAA, training adaptations of that book were enthusiastically received by afterschool professionals. *Promoting Positive Behavior After School* is my attempt to give back to afterschool professionals by encapsulating the contents from the first book and the afterschool trainings into tips, frameworks, and strategies that will inform, reassure, and guide young program leaders encountering the same anxieties and vulnerabilities that I experienced years ago.

Purpose of This Book

Like *Promoting Positive Behaviors: An Elementary Principals' Guide to Structuring the Learning Environment*, this book is intended to support reflective professional growth of afterschool personnel by focusing on small, concrete, common factors of people management that, if left unattended over time, can erode the program culture and climate.[1] Inappropriate behavior of students is most always a result of adults not knowing what to do or how to do their jobs. Afterschool program leaders, especially site-directors, play a key role in establishing the program vision and structure, teaching the frontline adults, who in turn, instruct the students. The potential of every school, and every afterschool program, will be actualized when the adults come together, identify needs, share ideas, beliefs, and values, and adopt common expectations as norms.

Description of the Book

Promoting Positive Behaviors After School is organized in five sections, each a part of the afterschool program time of day (or year) in which students, without positive direction from adults, will often react to confusion in less than desirable ways. The five sections of the book are:

I – Beginnings/Transitions (The Day and the Year)
II – Instruction and Learning
III – Midpoints/Break Time/Meals & Snacks
IV – Second Half (After 5:00 p.m.)
V – Endings (Dismissal Time and Wrap-Up of the Year)

Within each section are short informational topics and strategies for consideration that support the program structure and management of students during specific times and locations. Each section concludes with a staff discussion guide which includes goals and indicators of observable adult and student behavior that support the development of positive behaviors. The book can be read in entirety or studied section-by-section, preferably by an entire staff during professional development trainings, and utilized in ways that help adults learn, understand, improve, and master their practice in uniform ways.

Intended Audience(s)

It is anticipated that readers of this book would include, but not be limited to:

- site-level afterschool directors and aspiring leaders.

[1] You are encouraged to utilize *The Afterschool Program Culture Survey*, Appendix 1

- afterschool program leaders (with overall program responsibilities).
- school principals and other school leaders who work with before and after school care programs.
- 21st CCLC program leaders, trainers, and consultants.
- early childhood program leaders.
- college and university instructors.
- professional association leaders.
- afterschool youth programs (YMCA, Boys & Girls Clubs, Parks & Recreation, 4-H, Faith-based Groups, etc.).

Why This Book Is Needed

If you ask aspiring teachers about their greatest area of concern, most likely they'll reflect on the feelings of inadequacy in managing classrooms. Despite efforts to revise and improve clinical experiences, practicums, student teaching, and other observations in classroom settings, classroom management has always been a challenge for many new teachers. It is often cited as a reason many leave the profession within five years.

It takes time to acquire and fine-tune student management skills while also managing other tasks and situations that occur. It requires commonsense, consistency, courage, collaboration, and a sense of fairness, and hours of deliberate practice to develop proficient, time-trusted abilities.

When the adults at specific afterschool program sites make time to meet, discuss their vulnerabilities and experiences with distress, listen, brainstorm and share ideas, then respectfully determine strategies to address concerns, both student and adult behaviors improve. Because program sites are so unique, it is impossible for this book or any other to provide a quick, easy road map of how to get kids to act in positive ways. This volume can, however, be a guidebook for any staff to use to identify specific issues and concerns, develop plans that can tackle negative situations, and together share responsibility for success.

If we allow ourselves to get the point where we think we have tried everything, we likely have reached a point of failure. In my experience, I've learned that adults who really know why they've chosen education as a career, and work together as a team with a shared vision, will never succumb to throwing in the towel. Yes, there will always be those individual kids who won't respond to your directions or expectations, and they will test you to your limit. But will you cast any individual with severe issues aside or allow any one child to ruin learning experiences for others?

Afterschool programs with unruly kids most likely have a negative culture. A program's culture reflects its spirit. The program climate, not to be confused with culture, represents its attitude. Whenever professionals spend a significant amount of time together, they develop a common set of expectations which evolve into unwritten rules to which group members conform. Effective program staffs develop a common culture – a positive spirit - which is passed on to students who reflect that temperament through positive behaviors.

Despite our schools' and afterschool programs' unique differences (large/small, wealthy/poor, rural/urban, diverse/homogeneous) there are many commonalities. Readers are encouraged to reflect on the suggestions provided within this book and engage others in discussions about additional organizational structures that will enhance student learning opportunities in their programs. I have every confidence that given the time to learn, reflect, and grow, that afterschool professionals can manage kids in any setting, in any community, in positive ways. Nothing this important, however, can be achieved quickly. You must build a strong, effective culture every day. Celebrate small wins.

I hope this book helps you act, identify effective solutions to problems you might be experiencing, adapt, apply ideas, and realize the benefits that an improved structure has upon effectiveness and productivity.

People like structure because it provides information on how things should be done.

- Annette L. Breaux and Harry K. Wong (2003)

Structure:

a) the action of building something;
b) something made up of interdependent parts in a definite pattern of organization;
c) the arrangement of particles or parts in a substance or body;
d) the interrelation of parts as dominated by the general character of the whole;
e) the elements of an entity or the position of such elements in their relationship to each other.

Webster's Seventh New Collegiate Dictionary

Positive Behavior Interventions and Support (PBIS):

PBIS is a research-based, decision-making framework for implementing school and afterschool systems of behavioral support, in a tiered continuum based on student responsiveness to intervention. The goal is to help prevent and reduce undesired behavior and improve social and academic behavioral outcomes for all students in schools and afterschool programs. With PBIS, children and youth learn about behavior, just as they learn other subjects like math or science.

Explanation of Terms

Afterschool – In this book, the non-hyphenated use of afterschool designates an educational program, usually one occurring weekdays between 3 and 6 p.m. After school specifies a time of day. School age childcare and tutoring are often implied afterschool programs.

Site-Director – the individual responsible for a specific program location.

Program Director – the individual responsible for an entire program, which may include multiple sites.

Promoting Positive Behaviors After School

Structures that Support Adult and Student Performance within the School/Afterschool Culture

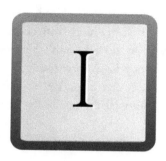

I

Beginnings/Transitions

Ideas and Advice That Support and Facilitate Smooth School-to-Afterschool Transitions, Efficacy of Time, and Effective Student Supervision

If you stumble out of the starting blocks,
you'll likely have a poor showing at the finish line.

- Paul Young

Introduction

Many factors impact the daily routine involving moving kids from their school to the afterschool program. Your program may be housed in the school, or students may walk or be transported to an off-school campus site. Regardless, how they are greeted, organized, treated, and supervised during this transition period contribute to a positive or negative experience. A bad start or transition can ruin a child's experience and that of numerous adults as well.

As you would learn in any music performance class, one of the most important notes of any song is the first. Believe it or not, playing it correctly requires hours of preparation and practice. Likewise, getting the start of an afterschool program off on the right note requires much preparation and practice. That planning involves attention to many small details each day, but good starts and transitions, especially those at the beginning of a school year or after long breaks also benefit from good training, reflection, and ongoing professional development. This chapter focuses on establishing positive behaviors related to student and adult safety, supervision, organization, communication, vision and mission, and other structures that impact the start of daily programming or planning that assures good starts at the beginning of the year.

1.1 – Teach and Clarify the Program Mission and Vision

Let's begin with the program mission and vision statements. If these don't exist, it would be good to spend time developing them before you begin working with kids. If your program is school-based, I recommend you adopt what is already in place and make it your own in collaboration with the school staff.

Why does your program exist? Why does the school exist? Ask those questions, and you'll likely receive blank stares or perhaps someone will ramble off a positive belief statement they've seen posted somewhere on a wall. Your school's mission (and that of your program) might outline a lofty goal or describe the offerings and educational goals. Your mission should explain why your program exists.

I submit that every school and afterschool program's mission is simply *to teach*. Your mission is your *why*. If what you do related to that *why* doesn't boil down to some form of teaching, you should reflect and ask why you are doing it.

Are snacks or meals related to your mission? Yes, they should be, as you and your staff should always be teaching the benefits of nutrition, health, manners, etiquette, and more during snack or meal time. Everything you do should be related to your *why* – *teaching*. If something doesn't, strongly consider not doing it, or better clarify how and why it does.

Viewed broadly, or simply as *teaching*, or *to teach*, the mission statement becomes easier for everyone to understand. The vision statement is more challenging to develop, communicate, clarify, and attain buy-in. The vision statement describes the clear and inspirational long-term desired change resulting from an organization or program's work. It should allude to what your program will look like, sound like, and feel like once you've taught all aspects of details related to the mission. How does the change you envision occurring unfold within the next week, month, year, and beyond? How do the stakeholders in your program understand that vision? Can they explain it? Do they buy-in? How about the students?

At West School, this became the first and most important part of collective work and transformation. Every staff member (certified and classified) needed to know why they were teaching every aspect of every minute detail (especially related to student behavior), how they were supposed to do it, and what outcomes they were expected to experience. Once we got everyone on the same bus, in the right seats, moving in the same direction, and sharing a positive vision, changes began occurring. We quickly discovered that the kids who were driving people crazy could be good if they were taught what they were supposed to in developmentally appropriate ways. Some staff members who wanted to sap energy from others had to be put off the bus and some new ones were invited on. I had to drive the bus, but always with the assistance and input of the passengers. Our bus existed to teach, and my job was to drive us to where we needed to go. Finding and choosing the right road to travel was hard work, but exciting once we knew we were on the right one.[2]

Again, there were some energy sappers. Everyone had to fight a tendency to look elsewhere for help or to push responsibility onto others. We had to avoid self-pitying comments that started like these:

- If we only had…
- If our program could…
- If parents would just…
- If we had people like…

Time spent discussing and clarifying your *why*, your mission, is worthwhile. Involve all your stakeholders, including parents, and even students who are developmentally able to understand and contribute to the discussion.

---

[2] Read Jon Gordon's *The Energy Bus: 10 Rules to Fuel Your Life, Work, and Team with Positive Energy.* (2007). Hoboken, NJ: John Wiley & Sons.

The vision needs to be discussed and clarified continuously. The program vision must be taught.

Mission	Vision	Values	Goals
Why your program exists.	What your program will become	How you behave and work toward the vision	The aspirations that mark your progress
Purpose of program	The future	Shared commitments	Targets and timelines
Clarifies priorities	Requires clarity and directions	Guide the group behavior	Actualized priorities

When your values align with your actions… you are authentic. It's that simple.

- Dr. Danny Steele

@SteeleThoughts

1.2 – Define Discipline and Punishment

One of the most important tasks to accomplish before your program begins is to define, as an entire staff, the terms *discipline* and *punishment.* Do your adults bring preconceived opinions that they assume mean the same, or do they differ? In your staff development activities, without setting any type of parameters, pose the question. See what results you receive.

Discipline should be viewed as a positive method of teaching young children self-control, confidence, and responsibility. Kids in your program must be taught what behavior is okay and what is not okay. You must teach, encourage, and model appropriate behavior.

The term *disciple* originates form the Greek and generally refers to "one who engages in learning through instruction from another, a pupil or apprentice."[3] It enters the English language from the Latin *discipulus* meaning a

[3] Danker, Arndt, W., W., Bauer, W., & Gingrich, F. W. (2000). A Greek-English lexicon of the New Testament and other early Christian literature (3rd ed). Chicago: University of Chicago Press. p. 609.

learner. In today's world, *discipline* means to train or develop by instruction, or training that corrects, molds, or perfects the mental faculties or moral character.[4]

Punishment is quite different from discipline. Many adults think of punishment in a physical sense as spanking, hitting, or causing pain. But it can also be viewed as disapproval, isolation, or shaming. Punishment focuses on past misbehavior and does little to help a child behave better in the future. Punishment instills a penalty. It focuses on making a child suffer for breaking the rules. Discipline is about teaching a child how to make better choices.

It is imperative that your staff's definitions of discipline and punishment be aligned with that of your students' school and that you communicate your definitions to parents. This is an important staff development topic. Discipline is proactive, rather than reactive. It prevents many behavior problems and it ensures kids are actively learning from their mistakes.

The word discipline comes from the word disciple. Discipline means "to train or bring a state of order."

1.3 – Develop a Code of Conduct

If there were ever opportunities to receive professional development for my staff, I tried to take advantage. One of the best outcomes of my school's involvement in the Ohio Classroom Management Project was the development of a Code of Conduct.

Previously, teachers worked with a typical list of classroom rules and adhered to general schoolwide norms (walk on the right, don't run in the halls, etc.) but inconsistently taught them. This training opportunity allowed a representative team to work off-site with groups from across the state to reflect, share and learn new ideas, and formulate a schoolwide student management plan. Credit a hardworking staff for their insight in realizing that less could be more.

4 4 Webster's Seventh New Collegiate Dictionary.

Rather than reworking old rules, our team agreed that a short, simple code that addressed universal goals and aspirations would work better. Fortunately, our school name involved only four letters which provided direction and an outline for the code.

West School Code of Conduct

W - Work for Quality
E - Earn Respect
S - Safety First
T - Treat Others Kindly

Once we explained the purpose of the code, explained how it would be used, and attained staff buy-in, we shared with it with the parent organization who immediately endorsed it. Then we convened an assembly of staff and students where we taught the four important concepts through dramatic role play, music, and any other format we could develop.

I reinforced expectations by talking about what I envisioned during the daily morning announcements. We made signs and posted them throughout the school. The code became visible on the website and the newsletter. It spread.

As principal, my disciplinary routine changed from issuing negative consequences to reteaching expectations aligned with the code, which students were expected to have memorized and be able to explain to me. After reviewing the student's offense as part of their office referral or due-process hearing, my first question was "What part of the code of conduct did you mess up?" Most always, students knew what they had done wrong, could verbalize their mistakes, and offer a plan of personal improvement. I told them I expected them to make better choices, follow the code, avoid the same mistake so they would never have to be referred to me again. Within a couple months, the office was mostly vacated, students were learning and responding, teachers were teaching, and my time was free to focus on other things.

My colleagues in other schools took note. Many tried to replicate our results. Those who internalized the concepts, committed to the process, and devoted time to training staff, saw results. One mentee, upon being named principal of another nearby school, rearranged the concepts into TEAM and still benefits from a code of conduct today.

Any School/Afterschool Program Code of Conduct

T – Treat Others Kindly
E – Earn Respect
A – Always Work Hard
M – Maintain Safety

Again, if your program is school-based, align your code with what students are taught during school. If one doesn't exist, find a way to work with the principal and staff to develop one. If you operate an independent program, delve into this process, learn all you can about schoolwide student management, be creative, and develop a code that you can own and get your stakeholders to adopt. Stay with it. Success comes from constant attention, teaching, and celebration of progress.

Successful Student Management Involves:

1) **Knowing and being able to explain the difference between good and bad.**
2) **Teaching students what good is and what it means in many forms (role play, drama, etc.).**
3) **Intervening (reteaching) when things are bad.**
4) **Celebrating success (praise) when things are good.**

1.4 – Build Relationships

Education researcher, Robert Marzano, observes that "positive relationships between teachers and students are among the most commonly cited variables associated with effective instruction. If the relationship is strong, instructional strategies seem to be more effective."[5]

[5] Relating to Students: It's What You Do That Counts, ASCD, 68 (*6*), pp. 82-83.

There is an increasing quantity of books, literature, and professional presentations on relationship building. New ideas are always helpful. Common actions that should be observable in your program might include:

- Adults greeting (and saying goodbye) students by name with a smile.
- Adults discovering and appealing to students' interests.
- Adults treating students with dignity and respect.
- Adults using a welcoming tone of voice, body language, and appropriate non-verbal communication.
- Adults sharing personal experiences with students.

The increased use of cell phones and other forms of electronic communication are often cited as reasons young people have weak relationship-building skills. Regardless of your perceptions, electronic communication, specifically text-based electronic communication, including e-mail, instant messaging, text messaging, and the social media networks of Twitter, Facebook, Instagram, Snapchat, and many more let young adolescents and teens do it all - text, chat, meet people, and share their pictures and videos - often under the radar of adults. Increasingly, interpersonal skill development – face-to-face talking – suffers. Even the young adults working in afterschool programs can benefit from being taught and learning strategies that gain attention of students and help build instant connections

Brothers Ori and Ram Brafman, in their book *Click: The Forces Behind How We Fully Engage with People, Work, and Everything We Do*,[6] outline important, somewhat instinctive strategies that everyone can develop to strengthen relationships. The click, which they describe as the magical moment when humans connect, can be accelerated by focusing on five areas of psychological forces:

1) <u>Similarity</u> (ex. birthdate, handedness, hobbies, birthplace, birth order color preference, favorite food, eyeglasses, etc.)
2) <u>Proximity</u> (closeness in space or time, preferential seating in class or meeting, regularity of contact with students; questioning)

---

[6] Brafman, O. & Brafman, R. (2010). *Click: The Forces Behind How We Fully Engage with People, Work, and Everything We Do*. New York: Crown Publishing.

3) Vulnerability (reading others' psychological cues and responding appropriately with a smile, eye contact, touch, or sense of safety)
4) Resonation (asking good questions; blending/adapting with another's rate of speech, body language, personal space)
5) Environment (Misery loves company, shared workspace, overcoming mutual adversity in a shared community).

Clicks are accelerated and strengthened when students talk and share personal information that is meaningful to them. Staff can initiate conversations and clicks by asking questions about:

- family (siblings, parents, grandparents, relatives, etc.).
- school or work (interests, challenges, strengths & weaknesses).
- hobbies (special interests, spending free time).
- culture (movies, sports, music, television, foods, books).

Have you ever fallen head-over-heals for another person? If you have, you understand the power of a clicking and how it shapes thinking, behavior, and emotions. When you click and connect with students, developing positive behaviors becomes much easier – and fun!

Try This! The 2 x 10 Relationship Builder

If you have a child who does not easily connect and has few positive relationships with other students or adults, invite him to spend 2 minutes each day, 10 days in a row with you (or any adult), *just to talk*. Engage the child in conversation and allow her to lead the direction of the conversation. Use the clicking skills listed above to build connections. Most often, after 10 days of positive attention, the relationship will have improved.

Modified from Educational Leadership, Sept. 2016, 74 (1), pp. 84-85.

Which Approach Works Best?

1. High Standards of Behavior Generate Better Relationships
2. Strong Relationships Generate Higher Standards of Behavior

The most common reasons children resort to fighting is because of their frustration and inability to manage their emotions when faced with teasing, disagreements over aspects of games, group inclusion or exclusion, unprovoked assaults, and dominance disputes.

Increasing numbers of children experience toxic stress in reaction to the trauma in their lives. Many do not know how to handle their emotions and deal with conflict with their peers or adults. They must be taught these skills. Many of their parents also lack coping skills. Hurt people will hurt other people. Little will lessen their pain and help improve behavior until a positive relationship has been formed between a caring adult and the child.

1.5 – Develop a Staff and Student Handbook

Likely, your program already has a student-and-staff handbook. Perhaps they are two separate documents. Upload the documents on your website. If they do not exist, contact your school principal for a copy of the school handbook which you could adapt, or check with your professional association for templates or referrals to quality programs that will likely, if asked, share theirs with you.

Prior to the start of your program, make sure handbooks are updated. Contents should be reviewed minimally once a year. The handbook should contain guidance and answers to parents' most frequent questions. Students, staff, substitutes, parents, and volunteers will benefit from the information, and the handbook help them understand how decisions are made. Information should be included that addresses the following:

- student enrollment processes, arrival, departure, release and withdrawal.
- homework policies, procedures, and expectations.
- general considerations for student safety and welfare while attending your program.
- emergency drills and evacuation procedures.
- disciplinary procedures, due process, and conflict resolution.
- policies on harassment and discrimination.
- child abuse and neglect definitions and reporting procedures.
- policies or dangerous weapons, drugs, social media usage, etc.
- standards for grooming, behavior, and self-responsibilities.
- procedures for reporting attendance, illness, absence, distributing medications, and dealing with emergencies.
- parental involvement, special programs, visitations, and volunteer opportunities.
- meals and snacks.
- program costs.

How does a student/staff handbook promote positive behavior? It provides important information in a uniform manner, outlines expectations and explains procedures. Left unaddressed, questions and concerns will emerge. A well-drafted student/staff handbook has other benefits, including:

- legal protection.
- clarity of your program mission, vision, values, and goals.
- guidance for employees.
- compliance with state and federal laws.
- an orientation tool for students and their families.
- specification for handling conflict disputes.

1.6 – Structure Effective Meetings

Nothing frustrates adults more than the leader arriving late to a meeting. Worse is being required to attend a scheduled meeting without an agenda where little is accomplished. People deservedly become irritated when the pace of meetings bog down and extend past the scheduled time.

Adults spend a considerable amount of time in program-related meetings and training. Leadership for these gatherings is best shared by all staff. To ensure that meetings produce results, prepare an agenda (see figure 1.6) and distribute it electronically in advance. Meetings will be most effective when those in charge of planning them consider the following planning tips.

Planning Tips

- Provide written notice to those who are invited or expected to attend.
- Adhere to the starting and ending time. Set discussion time limits.
- Establish group norms about prompt arrival, respect for others when brainstorming, sharing and critiquing ideas, and discussing topics.
- Delineate responsibilities for facilitating, reporting information, timekeeping, taking minutes, process evaluating, etc.
- Establish expected outcomes (decision, debate, discuss, share, etc).
- Determine in advanced how and when decisions will need to be made.
- Develop follow-up plans when necessary.
- Evaluate meetings from time to time for effectiveness.

Don't have meetings unless there is a good reason to have one. Meeting for the sake of meeting hardly ever produces an effective meeting.

The majority of meetings should be discussions that lead to decisions.
- Patrick Lencioni

Figure 1.6

Sample Staff Meeting Agenda

	Attendance P=Present A=Absent			
Date:	*John*	P	*Joey*	A
Time:	*Jane*	P	*Jeanelle*	P
Place:	*Jill*	P	*Julie*	P

Time	**Topic**	**Person Responsible**	**Preparation needed**	**Action or Type of Decision**	**Outcome** ***(to be completed by note-keeper)***
2:00	Gathering, greetings, Agenda approval,	Site-Director	Prompt arrival; agree to meeting norms	Approval of agenda	
2:03	Parent Pickup Procedures	Site-Director	Ideas, brainstorm	Staff review of data	
2:10	Talent Show	Ms. Jones	Review draft program	Clarity of roles, input	
2:25	Weekly Nuts and Bolts; Information; Expectations	Site-Director	Previous staff bulletins	Sharing of information; Delegation of tasks	
2:35	Code of Conduct	All Staff	Review	Recognition of strengths	
2:40	Wrap up Next mtg.	Site-Director			

Planning Tips

- Create a template starting by inserting a table into a Word document. Chose landscape layout for more room from left to right.
- The meeting note-keeper (assigned) simply uses the agenda as the format for completing meeting notes (or minutes) in the right-hand column (Outcome).
- Assign a timekeeper to keep everyone on schedule and pace.
- Schedule the next meeting before ending the current one.
- Sync your electronic calendars.

1.7 – The Staff Huddle

As a typical day unfolds, the program director likely becomes aware of information about students, events, activities, or priorities that all staff should know. When staff are purposefully, or even inadvertently left in the dark, it is a natural response for negativity to emerge. To avoid that, a simple, five or ten-minute huddle, during which internal information is shared coupled with an open exchange of concerns, can minimize confusion and boost team morale.

It is easy for a site-director to get swept up in multi-tasking activities of phone calls, emails, reports, and routine paperwork that causes a neglect of effective communications. Some staff will be hesitant to speak with you if they think they will interrupt. The daily huddle provides them an opportunity to communicate, ask questions, raise concerns, and hear first-hand the priorities that must be addressed that day.

For the huddle to be most effective, follow these tips:

- all program staff must attend.
- share good news to start the huddle.
- facilitate each staff member's sharing on a personal level.
- document what is discussed, provide feedback, and follow up.
- don't discuss negative personnel issues, conduct them one-on-one.
- avoid subsequent interruptions during programming.

The Daily Huddle Outline

1. Attendance & greeting
2. Positive warm-up
3. Announcements
4. Open discussion, raising of concerns,
5. Response to questions
6. Clarification of vision
7. Wrap up, assignments

Whether your program is a stand-alone or part of a multi-site organization, a written memo used as a follow-up to the staff huddle is helpful. A weekly memo should include important events and dates, especially those happening weeks in the future that require the staff's attention and special preparation. Also, use the memo to reinforce expectations, inform, and praise.

Good planning helps everyone approach their work positively. Utilize a form, as shown in Figure 1.7, to help organize the week.

Figure 1.7

<table>
<tr><th colspan="6">WEEKLY WORK OUTLINE</th></tr>
<tr><td colspan="3">Priority Tasks
1.
2.
3.</td><td colspan="3">Priority Calls to Make
1.
2.
3.</td></tr>
<tr><td colspan="2">Staff Contacts
☐
☐
☐
☐</td><td colspan="2">Student Observations
☐
☐
☐
☐</td><td colspan="2">Reports Due
1.
2.
3.</td></tr>
<tr><th colspan="6">TO DO LIST</th></tr>
<tr><td colspan="3">______________________
______________________</td><td colspan="3">______________________
______________________</td></tr>
</table>

1.8 – Plan for Effective Play Area Supervision During Transitions

Playground supervision should never be taken lightly. It should always be a topic of every staff's continuous improvement planning. Kids benefit from movement and exercise outdoors between school and afterschool.

Depending on where you live and work, the weather can vary and possibly reach extremes. Weather-related issues can become stressful, inconvenient, and a cause of negative behavior unless you learn to accept change in a positive way. Weather extremes can potentially create numerous challenges for teachers, paraprofessionals, afterschool program staff and directors, and principals – anyone with responsibility for playground supervision. The leadership style of the school principal sets the tone for everything at the school and can empower or stagnate the best ideas and efforts of the afterschool staff. For example, in school-based programs, if the principal prepares and takes weather-related issues in stride, so will the afterschool staff, students, and parents. Plan for all probable conditions during transitions – extreme cold, heat, rain, winds, thunderstorms, tornados, earthquakes, and threats from intruders.

Plan for effective play area supervision. Spend adequate time with the entire staff discussing expectations for both students and adults. Assure that all adults responsible for playground supervision understand their responsibilities. Then, **Do** the plan for a designated amount of time. At a designated point in the year, **Study** the results, then **Act** on recommended and agreed upon changes **(Plan, Do, Study, Act -- PDSA)**. Plan for the inside supervision of children when it rains. When it is extremely cold, develop a plan and designate space to supervise the children who will inevitably be dropped off before the designated time. Your plan will never pass public relations standards if children are refused entry and left outside in the cold. Each school campus has unique parameters, characteristics, and challenges that require your staff to address.

Whenever possible, children need time to run and play and to interact in socially acceptable ways with each other and adults. Don't short-change children's playtime. Considering that the number of overweight children (and adults) is steadily increasing, take advantage of every minute to engage students (and yourself) in physical activity. Are students allowed to run and play prior to the entrance bell? Must they be closely managed to control fights? Do they run free (and perhaps wild?) or are rules and guidelines enforced that create order and safety? Focus on creating structures during playtime that allow opportunities for strenuous activity. Numerous studies show than an increase in students' stamina can lead to higher achievement levels in the classroom.

Without the establishment of limits and expectations, expect chaos. Create a kid-friendly play area but maintain adult control. To do that, engage with students while they are playing. Students love it when adults talk with them, play games, walk and run, and smile. Remember, the adults are role models for the playground.

Planning Tips

- Determine the environmental conditions under which students can play.
- Assure that all staff members understand who makes decisions and why.
- Model expectations of playground (outdoor) behavior and be attentive to potential dangers. Adults should have unobstructed visual coverage of all parts of the playground. They should also assure that all visitors, parents, or volunteers have obtained authorization to be on the playground. Any intruders or suspicious activities in the vicinity of the playground should be reported to proper authorities.
- Regularly inspect the play equipment and document the results.
- Assure that plans have been reviewed by local authorities, school district officials, and communicated to parents.

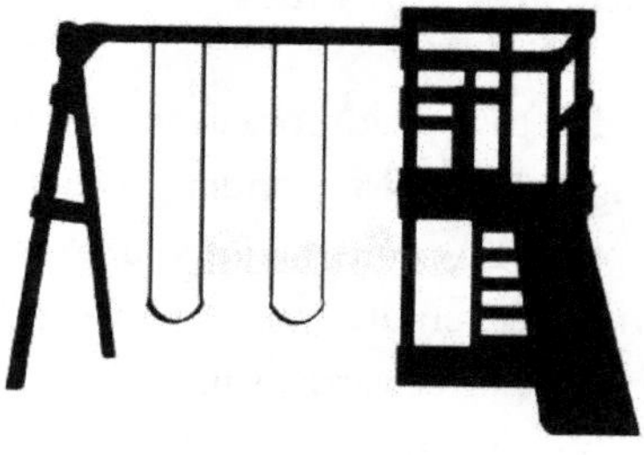

1.9 – Involve Students and Volunteers with Transition Supervision

Whether or not play time is scheduled, students can be assigned roles and tasks during school-to-afterschool transition that help them gain ownership, a sense of recognition, and feeling of accomplishment. Like the school safety patrol, assisting adults with transition activities provides a service learning opportunity for students.

Planning Tips

- Assign a staff member to train and monitor the students as they perform their duties.
- Enlist the support of adult volunteers who might also assist with collection of needed books and materials, which when left at school, can become a cause of negative behavior during the program.
- Engage the cooperation and support of the principal and school staff in sorting program students from those leaving school for other destinations.
- Provide all regular and substitute personnel with rosters, contact information, and other important information pertaining to students.
- Equip staff with walkie-talkies or cell phones to maintain communications among adults and the school office.

Effective adult training and experience with creating an upbeat, welcoming transition experience sets the stage for positive learning experiences and personal responsibility.

1.10– Teach Students How to Form Lines

It never seems to fail that children will antagonize each other, physically or verbally, when forming a line. No wonder, sometimes, that certain adults continue to do the same. You've watched adults in line at the store?

We assume young children are taught to form lines in preschool. They likely are, as well as every year afterwards. Once they've learned, however, they benefit from constant monitoring and reteaching of expectations. Left unwatched, bullies will begin their dastardly deeds, or students push and shove, and soon the adult is forced into reactionary mode that often is anything but positive. Proximity to children who are prone to initiate interpersonal conflicts can often prevent problems from ever developing.

Planning Tips

- Program staff must adopt a proactive and preventative approach to solving problems when forming student lines. Positive considerations work much better than always reacting to what students have done.
- Adults should position themselves near line formations so that they can always be seen and heard by the children.
- If possible, paint or mark a designated line on the ground or floor where each group of students should congregate and form a line. If desired, structure and space a consistent length to the line.
- Assign students who pose behavioral challenges with a designated position within the line close to where the supervising adult will be.
- Teach children how to maintain personal space between each other.
- Teach students when it is appropriate to talk, when it is not, and what level of voice to use in various settings.

All staff members must collectively envision the standards of acceptable supervisory performance and consistently adhere to them. Likewise, they should practice with students until appropriate behaviors standards are observable each day. Vary your procedures, students' order in line, and any other aspects of queuing lines that might become stale over time. Never stop teaching and reinforcing expectations. Set a positive, welcoming tone. Treat children with respect, and they will learn to return it the same.

1.11 – Communicate Plans & Build Relationships with Parents

One of the most stressful time of day for working parents is when school is dismissed and their children must be transported home or to some other destination. Mornings are busy and often hectic, and pick-up plans can change.

How smoothly transitions are planned, communicated, and executed can be a source of comfort – or a time of stress, concern, and negative outcomes.

Planning Tips

Every school and afterschool program should have numerous, noticeable indicators that parents are welcome at school. These indicators should include pleasant, parent name recognition from all staff, not just the secretary.

- Place welcoming signs at main entrances.
- Develop a procedure for greeting parents and meeting their needs in an efficient manner.
- Develop a reception area with coffee, tea, and other niceties.
- Create a parent resource room.
- Communicate the transition plan to parents.
- Assure parents of student safety precautions.
- Make sure all staff, as well as school officials, are informed of any changes to routine procedures.

Review your program's website. Is it parent friendly? Does it provide current information that successfully markets your program? Is it a source of positivity and pride?

Each staff member must embrace a program commitment that focuses on parent reception and positive involvement. Continuously assess your practices and services. Would you want to be a parent of a child in your program?

Most afterschool programs with stellar reputations have earned parents' trust and respect for their initiatives focused on public relations and safety, especially related to concerns that might pertain to the transition from school to afterschool. The most successful and longest-lasting results are achieved and sustained when each staff member routinely and genuinely greets each individual parent with respect, conveys concern for all children, encourages a partnership, and wears a warm smile. Positive overtures during the first few days of programming that become overshadowed by less hospitable habits due to a busy routine are erased by a climate of negativity. When a staff comes together and sustains efforts to greet parents each day, public relations, communication, support, and involvement increases. Happy parents will advocate for an afterschool program that they like as one of choice.

Communicating with Parents

No matter how many attempts at communication you make with parents, some just do not seem to be capable of any responsibility. Would you choose the staff member's first or second response to this parent's email?

Parent: Skippy tells me he is supposed to wear a costume for the program tonight, but he never brought one home. I do remember paying the fee for it when he registered for the program. Do you have the costume?

Staff Member's 1st Reply: WHERE HAS YOUR CHILD BEEN FOR THE LAST 6 WEEKS WHEN I SENT THE COSTUMES HOME AND WE'VE TALKED ABOUT THE UPCOMING PROGRAM ALMOST DAILY?!?!?!?!?!?

Staff Member's 2nd Reply (after deleting the first): Good morning. I cannot imagine how this happened. I sent them home weeks ago, and I have reminded students multiple times since then about making sure things fit. I have everything here. We will make sure he is good to go for tonight. The only issue might be his pants, as they most likely need to be hemmed. See you this evening. Have a relaxing day.

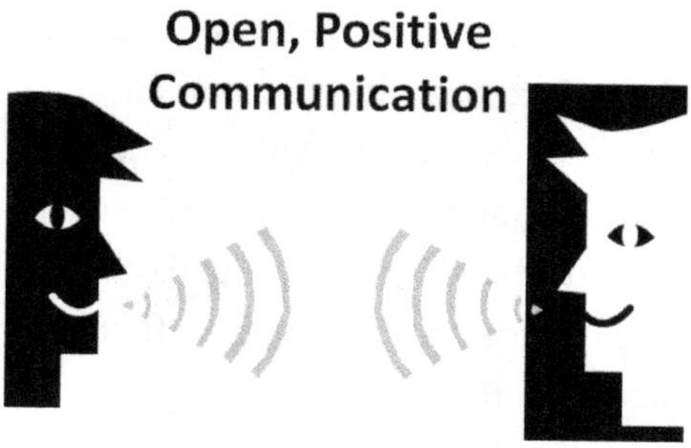

1.12 – Teach Children to Move Quietly Through Hallways

Getting children to one place from another without being loud and disruptive can be a constant challenge. Some adults can supervise this task effectively while others cannot, typically because they approach the task less attentively. Consistent staff supervision is important. Proactive attention to small details will result in much less stress and behavioral problems.

Planning Tips

- Envision the results you want and expect to see and hear them.
- Observe master teachers while they supervise line movements.
- Teach children the appropriate behaviors they are expected to display during the task.
- Assign a line leader and a "caboose."
- Selectively place students in the line for effective interactions.
- Practice with the children.
- Continuously monitor with eyes and ears.
- Expand lines no further than a supervising adult can see or hear.
- Align expectations with what occurs during the school day.
- Acknowledge the importance of managing this task as it relates to the overall effectiveness of student management.

If your program is housed in a school and teachers remain in it after hours while your program is in session, you'll gain "points" and respect if your students are supervised and managed effectively. Alignment and consistency matter. If kids are not allowed to run in the hallways or wear hats in the building during the day, you'll only encounter problems from the teaching staff if you choose to allow them to do otherwise.

1.13 – Secure Your Program Area

Once the students have arrived at your program site, secure it by locking the doors. Post signs indicating the state code that limits outside access except at the main entrance. Inform all staff and parents of the security policy and its rationale. Instruct students not to open doors and allow entry to professionally dressed men and women who "look like they have business here".

In school-based programs, locking the doors may be somewhat problematic. If there are other after-school activities and events that occur at the same time, especially where the public might be on campus, locking doors might be impractical. Work with the school principal or designee to address concerns and formulate a security plan.

When possible, lock the doors to protect children from uninvited outside intruders. All staff must be alert to suspicious activities. Teach students how to respond appropriately in situations of emergency. It just makes good sense.

1.14 – Teach Etiquette & Dress Codes

If the school your students attend has a dress code, enforce it in your program. If there isn't one, consider writing one and adding it to your student/staff handbook. Many schools and districts adopt uniform policies. Dress codes must meet legal standards and students' constitutional rights. The courts also uphold the right and responsibility of administrators to maintain order and safety within the scope of the school day and year. Personal attire that creates disruption can be prohibited.

Most visitors will tell you that order and discipline are better in afterschool programs with a dress code. Additionally, if the staff dresses professionally, a positive message is conveyed to students and parents. Teach students to be polite, use the words *please* and *thank you*, and demonstrate other common acts of kindness toward their peers and adults.

If the school the students attend has a "no hat" rule, enforce it in your program. For older generations, removing hats in schools was a common rule of etiquette. Print the rules of etiquette in handbooks, at entry locations, in newsletters, concert programs, and elsewhere for the public's information. Clarify the expectations and their justification in a positive manner. Most people will applaud your efforts.

1.15 – Greet Students by Name and Look Them in the Eye

People love it when you can address them by their name – first as well as last. When they recognize that you also know something about them, it further validates their individuality and strengthens your relationship with them. Students gain your acceptance and feel they belong in the program. Work at remembering names by developing mind association games, looking for cues in classrooms, reviewing each child's grade card, spending time looking at class pictures and seating charts, mentally reviewing names while observing in classrooms, and saying names over and over. For those few who act out frequently, you'll know too well. Sometimes, they distinguish themselves and everyone knows them by only *one* name. Unfortunately, the well-behaved students, those who complete their work, follow the rules, and meet expectations are those whose names we sometimes fail to learn.

The more effectively you can greet students by using their name and make eye contact with them, the more they will reciprocate. It's usually not hard to make connections with kids. Adults must be willing to take the first step.

People appreciate the effort it requires to know names. Parents will be impressed when they observe, especially in large schools, when staff members greet children by name and ask questions about a sibling or an activity associated with the child or family. Usually, the child beams. It makes their day.

It may be surprising, but young children sometimes don't know the last name of their friends – even their family members. They just know the grandmother as "Gigi". Everyone in the school will benefit from learning first and last names,

Site-directors have great influence in their programs. Knowing names of people in the school community is a critical skill in expanding that influence.

1.16 – Check Mail and Messages At Least Twice Daily

Paperless communication via email is effective, less expensive, and more rapidly disseminated – only if the afterschool staff is trained to regularly check for messages. Establish a norm of two reviews of the inbox each day – upon report to work and before the end of the workday for frontline staff, more often for full-time employees. For some, however, email becomes addictive. Avoid the tendency to run to the computer every time an audible sound indicates a new message. Turn that mechanism off!

Not all communication can be disseminated in a paperless manner. There will always be mail, handwritten phone messages, handouts for staff and parents, and special deliveries placed in staff mailboxes that need to be picked up and attended to regularly.

Staff members should strive to respond to email communication within 24 hours. Failure to reply in a timely manner results in negative culture and program reputation.

Summary

Afterschool programs have numerous structures that should be addressed by all staff members to assure consensus and uniform understanding and fulfillment of expectations for getting the year and each day afterward off to a smooth start. What has been discussed in Chapter 1 is simply a start. Add to the list to meet your unique setting and needs.

Typically, there are three influential groups among professional staffs that can limit others' ability to establish structure. They are:

1. the program leader or others within the administrative team that fail to establish a vision and clear expectations.
2. the "old guard" among staffs that typically shut their doors, fail to work with a team, have differing levels of expectations, and show little interest in assuming responsibility for reflection and program improvement.
3. the "rookies" who may or may not understand the importance of structure. Their ideas and habits are still in formative stages and sometimes not aligned with best practices of the program's operation. They need encouragement, support, and a safe environment to make mistakes, grow, and learn best practice.

Utilize the checklist that follows, as well as those in subsequent chapters, as a guide to reflect and assess the organizational cohesiveness of your program, to determine strengths and weaknesses, establish goals and assess current practice in your setting. The checklists can be used to summarize and reflect on the key points described in each chapter. They will help the reader or study groups determine what is applicable (or not) in other settings and identify other components for unique school environments. The practice of analyzing adult performance behaviors and the establishment of site norms will improve productivity and make the work environment better for everyone.

Setting & Communicating Expectations

- Keep to a small number of general rules that students understand and can easily recall.
- Emphasize appropriate behavior.
- Post rules in the classroom.
- Monitor student behavior constantly and reteach expectations frequently.
- Never issue consequences you are unwilling to actuate.
- Align expectations with program code of conduct.

Good Praise, Bad Praise

Effective	***Ineffective***
Immediate	Infrequent
Selective & Focused	Random & Indiscriminate
Specific	Generalized
Sincere	Lackluster
Based on effort	Based on comparison
Enlightening	Uninformative
Addresses competence	Meaningless
Intrinsic	Extrinsic
Conditional	Unconditional
Genuine	Fake

Checklist # 1 - Beginnings/Transitions—Structural Analysis and Assessment

Goal 1	Indicators	A	B	C	D	NA
There is an effective supervision plan for students during the transition from regular school to the afterschool program.	a) An adequate number of adults are in place to supervise students.					
	b) Plan includes accommodations for weather.					
	c) Attendance recording procedures are designated and closely followed.					
	d) Transition plan allows physical play time for children.					
	e) Adults interact with children and teach expectations.					
	f) The staff leads games and recreation activities.					
	g) A plan exists for getting homework, supplies, and materials prepared for afterschool.					
	h) A supervisory plan exists while students use the restrooms.					
	i) The school operates from a mission and with supportive vision statements.					

Goal 2	Indicators	A	B	C	D	NA
There is an effective plan for greeting parents and students.	a) Parent welcome signs are visible.					
	b) Staff members speak to parents.					
	c) Staff members know names of students and parents.					
	d) Teachers greet their classes at the gathering area.					
	e) Preventative problem solving is observed.					
	f) Phone calls (absences) and messages are responded to each day.					
	g) Student incentives are observable.					

Checklist # 1 - Beginnings/Transitions—Structural Analysis and Assessment

Goal 3	Indicators	A	B	C	D	NA
The supervisory plan focuses on teaching positive behaviors and meeting student needs.	a) Staff supervises students during the formation lines effectively.					
	b) Students respond quickly and appropriately to directions from staff.					
	c) Minimal time is wasted moving students from one point to another.					
	d) Movement through hallways is quiet and orderly.					
	e) Organization is evident.					
	f) Home–school-afterschool program communication plans are in effect.					
	g) Snacks/meals are provided.					
	h) A dress code is enforced.					

Goal 4	Indicators	A	B	C	D	NA
There is an effective plan for safety and security.	a) Play space is routinely inspected and meets safety standards.					
	b) Doors are secured, locked, and unauthorized people prevented access during school/afterschool hours.					
	c) Program organization/environment displays "curb" appeal.					
	d) Program environment is well maintained and clean.					

Goal 5	Indicators	A	B	C	D	NA
The vision of the afterschool program's transition time, supervision, and common expectations are communicated.	a) Vision and expectations are communicated in various forms by principal/afterschool program director.					
	b) Daily announcements are made.					
	c) Parents are made aware of expectations.					
	d) Parents are welcomed at the afterschool program.					
	e) All staff cooperates to avoid wasted time.					

Checklist # I - Beginnings/Transitions—Structural Analysis and Assessment						
Goal 6	**Indicators**	**A**	**B**	**C**	**D**	**NA**
There is evidence of staff planning and adherence to norms of structure and organization.	a) Effective meetings are conducted.					
	b) Data shows that an effective intervention process is in place.					
	c) Planning occurs and achieves desired results.					
	d) Data is used to make informed programmatic change.					

Summary Notes:

Identified Norms of Afterschool Program Structure:

Areas of Strength:

List… (ex. I-1b, etc.)

Targeted Areas for Improvement:

List… (ex. I-2b, etc.)

Adult Behavioral Norms Needed to Achieve Expectations:

Recommendations:

II

Instruction and Learning

Ideas and Advice That Enhance Instruction and Increase Student Achievement

Always desire to learn something useful.

- Sophocles

Introduction

Once the transition from school has occurred and students and adults have settled into your program setting, other considerations for developing and sustaining positive behavior an effective program structure become the focus. Do all the adults have a common understanding and expectation of what it means to actively engage students in learning? Do all students have a sense of security and belonging? Is instructional time being maximized rather than being lost to unexpected distractions? Do students have needed books and materials? How is homework handled? Is there a fool-proof plan for helping kids get homework turned in to their teachers at school? Do substitutes know the expectations for their assignment? Do they know when and how to seek help? Do all staff members adhere to a level of mastery utilizing volunteers, supervising students outside their classrooms, administering a code of conduct, and planning effective lessons?

What follows in this chapter, for individual and group consideration, are a sampling of structural issues that might occur during the first instructional block of the program (or year) that can potentially impede, or support, staff members' capacity to deliver engaging lessons and effectively manage their students.

2.1 – Supervise Student Transitions to and from Special Classes

Good lessons should not be interrupted by excessive noise or disruptions from unsupervised students. Lack of respect for other's work erodes the program culture. Adult supervision of students while moving to and from special classes and areas within your program should be established as a building norm. An effective plan for exchanging students preserves precious instructional time and reduces the stress of addressing inappropriate behaviors for everyone. Exchanging students and moving them from place to place with efficacy is an indicator of a disciplined staff.

Planning Tips

- Teachers should habitually walk their students to and from special classes, effectively supervising students and reinforcing expectations along the way.
- Punctuality should be observed. Nothing irritates a special resource teacher or volunteer more than another teacher's inability to watch a clock.
- Regular classroom and special education teachers must work together to assure an effective transition of students between their instructional areas.
- Adults know which students are most apt to initiate inappropriate behavior in lines while moving from place to place. Proactively place those students in a position where they can be effectively supervised.

Don't lose track of time. Adults who complain that they have inadequate amounts of instructional time must first assure they aren't wasting it!

What Would You Do?

Alice is a mid-50s, certified teacher who works in the afterschool program to support students' reading and writing development. She recently retired from public school. During the day, she cares for her aging parents who live with her. By all appearances, she is a pleasant woman and was a good teacher. When she retired, she was serving as a Reading Recovery instructor.[7]

Now, Alice works three hours each day with 12-15 fifth graders in a second-floor language arts resource room. At 5:00 p.m., she is scheduled to take those students to the first-floor media center where she works with a library aide to help them to learn and develop keyboarding and writing skills. Typically, however, she and her students arrive late. Often, a few of the students create a distraction along the way.

As the site-director, you happen upon Alice and her students in the hallway as she opens the door to escort them into the media center. You notice only six students with her. Then, looking down the hallway, you notice a straggler. As you continue walking down the hallway, you notice another coming around a corner. Thirty steps further, you find two others arguing over a book on the staircase. After correcting the students, you decide to continue up the stairs to Alice's language arts resource room. There, you find the last two stragglers, and one of them is Skippy, who you are very familiar with because of Alice's (and other staff members') frequent behavioral referrals for your intervention.

This day, however, Skippy hadn't bullied anyone or created any distraction. But if he had, typically a student would have reported him to Alice, and she would have said, "Go to the office"!

As you (and your staff) reflect on this scenario, answer the following questions:

1. Is anything wrong?
2. Does anything need to be corrected?
3. How do any corrections need to occur?
4. What does the staff need to know and be able to do?
5. What should happen to Alice?
6. What should happen to Skippy?

---

[7] Reading Recovery is a widely researched intervention for young children having extreme difficulty with early literacy learning.

2.2 – Establish Procedures for Restroom Breaks

It is best that students use the restroom immediately after the school day during transition time. However, there will likely be some who will ask to use the restroom before the end of a learning activity or scheduled break period. These restroom breaks, if not well supervised, become moments when students play around, waste time, or misbehave. Supervision is never needed less – it is needed more!

Establish supervisory norms for this daily occurrence. Clearly teach the expectations and revisit the norms, particularly for new enrollees, several times throughout the program year to refresh common expectations and address concerns.

Planning Tips

- Schedule restroom breaks so that all classes won't congregate in a crowded corridor, overload the facilities, and waste time.
- Teach students to wash their hands and place paper towels in waste containers.
- Teach students to flush toilets and urinals.
- Teach students to use inside voices while in restrooms.
- Avoid sending all students, either gender, into a restroom, out-of-sight, at one time.
- Be selective about which students are allowed in the restroom at the same time. Don't allow bullies an opportunity to do their deeds!
- Develop an orderly and quick process of allowing students in and out of the restroom while others are washing hands and getting drinks. Send students into the restroom at staggered intervals or small groups and expect them back in a reasonable amount of time in the same order. Teach them to avoid loitering and mischief.
- Make sure soap is available in the restroom.
- Adults should not hesitate to step inside the restroom of their gender to observe student behavior and compliance with expectations. If men are few in numbers at your program, ask for help from male custodians, paraprofessionals, or volunteers.
- Make sure substitutes are aware of the restroom break plan.

Who is the More Capable Supervisor?

Staff Member A: Her third graders were scheduled for a restroom break. When the children arrived outside the restroom doors, she gave a verbal direction explaining how students were to enter the appropriate restroom, then walked down the hallway to speak with the custodian and the cook about a matter unrelated to the afterschool program. Five minutes later, she returned to discover that two boys had plugged a urinal full of toilet paper and it was overflowing water into the hallway.

Staff Member B: Her third graders were scheduled for a restroom break. When the children arrived outside the restroom doors, she gave a verbal direction for two or three students to enter each restroom while she continued teaching those who were waiting a turn. As the break time unfolded, she was observed asking follow-up questions related to the lesson she and her students had been discussing and interacting positively with all students.

Not surprisingly, it is Staff Member B. She has mastered what might appear to be the most insignificant routines and practices. She rarely, if ever, wastes time. Students also rarely, if ever, find themselves out from under her watchful eye. As a result, her students would never plug a restroom urinal. The most conscientious parents will do whatever they can to have their child assigned to Staff Member B. And kids prefer her to Staff Member A.

2.3 – Practice Entering and Leaving Assemblies

If you invite special speakers and presenters to visit your program, you don't want to be embarrassed by your students' behavior when they arrive for the activity or while the guest is talking. Presenters that routinely visit schools and afterschool programs will observe the student and staff entrance and preparation for the assembly. Some will share stories of when they were hardly able to speak over the noise from inattentive students. Those presenters likely formed a poor impression of the control and influence the site-director and staff. The students, perhaps not to blame, unfortunately acted as students will without structure and high expectations. Speakers are left with an unfortunate opinion of the program. Some choose never to return.

Planning Tips

- Disconnect or silence unnecessary, annoying loud bells and other distractions (ex. cell phones).
- Practice entering and leaving assembly areas with dignity and respect for guests.
- Plan restroom visits before assembly gatherings.
- The program leader, or designee, should monitor students and staff during the entrance and introduce the speaker.
- Assure that students know the appropriate voice for presentations, what to wear, how to sit and stay seated.
- If students must sit on hard floors, assure they have been cleaned.
- Items that might distract presenters or other students should be left out of the assembly area.
- Position students with special needs near adults.
- Develop a signal for quiet. Do not speak until all voices (student and adult) are silent.
- Teach students to make eye contact with presenters.
- Avoid excessive public announcements.
- Praise good behavior.
- Staff should remain for the assembly and model good listening skills.
- Staff should not congregate in the back of the room talking among themselves.
- At the conclusion the presentation, express gratitude toward the speaker and encourage students and staff to show their appreciation with respectful applause.
- An orderly dismissal should be conducted in a respectful manner.

Expect compliments when your students meet expectations. Realize that presenters will pass on the good news to their colleagues and to afterschool personnel in other programs.

2.4 – Assure That Substitutes Have Adequate Plans

If regular staff members must be absent, substitutes play an important role in providing continuity. For them to fulfill expectations successfully, they will need support and direction from regulars. Courteously welcome substitutes and assure that their questions are answered and that they understand their assignment.

Tips for Planning

Substitutes, especially those new to your program the first time, will benefit from various pieces of information which can be prepared in advance.

- Name(s) of go-to staff members.
- A building or program area map, diagram, or outline.
- Daily schedule.
- Information of location of restrooms, books, audio materials, computer operations and passwords, games, snacks, rosters with student contact information.
- Student snack and meal procedures.
- Play area supervision expectations, code of conduct, and needed rules.
- Lists of special staff duties and how to fulfill expectations for each.
- Emergency information explaining drills, plans, and procedures.
- Dismissal procedures, bus lists, parent pick-up procedures.
- Explanations/locations of adult needs (staff lounge, adult restrooms, lunch costs, contact people, time sheets, etc.)

Most importantly, there should be clear, detailed plans for substitutes to follow listing expectations for their work and student supervision. When they arrive at work, and the program staff is unprepared to assist them, they likely will not be as effective as they could be. When they experience a negative situation, they will talk about it. Kids will sense it, and when structures are weak, they will often act in inappropriate ways.

2.5 – Time-on-Task

No doubt, when more students are engaged in worthwhile tasks and demonstrate time-on-task behavior, the more they achieve. Students' attention spans vary, and for some, an environment without some form of predetermined restrictions may be less than adequate to meet their needs.

For most students without special needs, adults need to know how to provide directions, monitor work, avoid distractions and interruptions, and redirect when needed. Time-on-task is a complex topic that requires teachers to commit hours of practice to manage. It is important that afterschool program staff understand and develop skills to maximize time. When adult skills are weak, negative behaviors will emerge because students quickly become distracted and bored when the adult is off task. When school staff observe that time-on-task is less than adequate, afterschool programs are labeled as being little more than babysitting.

2.6 – Establish Protocols for Referring Students to the Site-Director

Does it bother you if a program director says, "Effective staff members hardly ever send students to my office?" It shouldn't, and adults who are skilled at motivating and engaging their students rarely find it necessary to do so. But kids will be kids. Despite best efforts, there are important reasons why kids should be referred to the office. Here are four:

1) <u>Personal injury or sickness</u>. If there is blood, the site-director and office staff should know about it. Anytime a child becomes sick, especially vomiting, staff must seek assistance. That doesn't mean a free pass or automatic office visit for any child that complains of an ache or pain. When that is allowed, every bored child will suddenly become afflicted with aches and pains.

2) Illegal or illicit behavior. If a staff member suspects drugs, weapons, theft, or other violations of the school, afterschool program, or school district's serious misconduct code, the site-director must know. Protecting a child or failing to report can be negligent – and disastrous.
3) Overt refusal to follow an adult's directions. No child has the right to ignore reasonable directions of an adult. The problem with implementing this guideline is establishing a common-sense level of understanding and tolerance among adults.
4) Danger or threat to other students. Children should not have their right to learn in a safe environment threatened by others. Often, challenging students require a more restrictive environment than an afterschool program might be equipped to provide. To provide an inclusive environment with adequate supports, the program leader must collaborate with school, community officials, and parents to make necessary provisions. No adult should be subjected to personal assault or injury from a student who, unprovoked and without just cause, maliciously attacks an adult or child with the intent to harm.

There can be other justifiable reasons to refer students for administrative support. The four listed above serve as a guide. Adults must learn how to pick their battles, continuously teach expectations, utilize their extensive repertoire of motivational techniques, know when to ignore, and engage most of the students all the time. They must understand that when they let down their guard, the kids will take advantage. When that begins to happen routinely, it should not be the site-director's job to fix the problem. Over time, it will become clear that site-director's job is to fix the adult, not the kids.

What Would You Do?

You work in the afterschool program. You are also a certified reading specialist. During state testing, you've been asked (and paid) to assist 5th grade teachers with the language arts test administration. The day of the test, you observe a teacher shake her head one unique way while Skippy is taking his test and looking at her. You don't think the teacher can see you observing this.

___ Anonymously report what you observed to the State Department of Education.
___ Report what you observed to the school's principal.
___ Report what you observed to your direct-report, the afterschool program site-director.
___ Discuss your concerns with the teacher.
___ Ignore it.

2.7 – Fully Utilize Volunteer Services

Volunteers are special people who can provide immeasurable resources to afterschool programs. They are deserving of great respect and gratitude. The way their time in your program is structured, managed, and assessed is an important consideration that should not be left at the discretion of individual staff members. Where there are systems in place to identify needs, solicit volunteers, train them, and listen to their concerns and ideas, volunteerism will flourish.

When developing a volunteer program, establish a guide or handbook (much like that prepared for substitutes). It should include:

- a list of common expectations and information available to all guests at the school and/or the afterschool program.
- detailed information outlining timeframes and the work or service to be provided.
- expectations related to background checks and confidentiality.
- information contained within a substitute handbook that would be pertinent to a volunteer.

Nothing will discourage the spirit of volunteerism more than the staff's failure to plan and prepare, establish clear expectations from the start, provide feedback, and be honest and accountable. Volunteers want assurance that their work is appreciated and contributing to a common good. Otherwise, they will feel their time is wasted.

Don't allow the contributions of volunteers to go unrecognized, even if some of them prefer otherwise. Volunteer recognition events need not be costly or extravagant – nor should they be limited only to annual events. The point is that every professional staff should find numerous ways to continuously express their gratitude to volunteers both individually and collectively.

2.8 – Schedule and Compensate Staff for Adequate Planning Time

Master teachers recognize the power of collective experience and wisdom and create ways to plan together. The best results are achieved when all the staff members who provide instruction for a grade level, including special resource teachers, plan for instruction and assessments together.

Planning Tips

- For unit planning or multi-day activities, agree upon a common planning time. Come prepared with necessary resources. Coordinate and plan alignment activities with school teachers when possible. Your goal should be to extend, enrich, and expand upon students' learning that has occurred in the regular school.
- Utilize a variety of data to drive instructional decisions, such as benchmark and chapter tests, standardized tests, writing samples, and observations in consultation with your students' regular school teachers.
- Coordinate lessons with the school's curriculum map which should be aligned with the district course of study and mandated tests. The map should list the essential concepts and standards that must be taught and learned at proficient levels by students.
- Invest in staff professional learning activities and consultants that produce results.

Afterschool professionals who plan together and stay together eventually get results and enjoy coming to work. Two heads are better than one. It is much easier to paddle a boat with several oars in the water than alone.

Summary

Chapter One dealt with structural concepts that could be planned and implemented at the beginning of a school year or the program day. In contrast, Chapter Two focused mostly on structural issues that support staff instructional practices and management of students within learning environments and areas of the program facility where they move about in groups or alone. Statements made in this chapter and throughout the book imply that higher levels of productivity are attainable when individual management capabilities are aligned throughout the program and with the students' school(s). All adults must work together from a common framework of behavior values and understandings. Together, items in this chapter (and those unique to your program) should be discussed.

Furthermore, many of the essays and stories affirm that adults play a key role in teaching children to display positive behaviors that lead to their success. Afterschool professionals who struggle to control students demonstrate varying degrees of incapacity that refrain students from attaining that success. Today, more than ever before, educators must be prepared and committed to improving their supervisory and management skills. They must be equipped with a repertoire of instructional methods and strategies that effectively address the diverse needs of students. They must reduce gaps of the slowest while simultaneously challenging the brightest. Those can be foreboding tasks for any individual. But practice and reflection provide opportunities to learn something new each new day (and year) as they unfold.

DiGiulio (2007) described three axioms for student success and positive classroom management:

1. Students who feel successful are seldom behavior problems.
2. To feel successful, students must actually be successful.
3. To actually be successful, a student must first do something of value.

The development of positive behaviors occurs on the front line. Students must recognize the adult in charge as the authority figure. When adults fail to establish positive connections, students will challenge and act out. If an adult is unable to handle challenges, her students will quickly surmise that she lacks backbone and control. When there is one weak link among the staff, and that weak link is allowed to persist, the opportunity for others to develop and work in a positive culture lessens.

The artistic aspect of teaching is likely what entices many young people to enter the profession. Most want to emulate a favorite teacher. But teaching is both an art and a science. The educational environment is always evolving. Change *can* be good, and it is a process. But no matter how things change, success and satisfaction are unattainable when the structural and physical dimensions of the learning environment are misunderstood or ignored.

Checklist # II - Instruction and Learning—Structural Analysis and Assessment						
Goal 1	**Indicators**	**A**	**B**	**C**	**D**	**NA**
Afterschool instruction is engaging, motivating, and inclusive.	a) Teachers/staff "wow" students, parents, and visitors.					
	b) Labels and turf issues are nonexistent.					
	c) Student behavioral problems are minimal.					
	d) Environment is quiet during instructional hours.					
	e) There are positive results from the implementation of a code of conduct.					
	f) Awareness of time on task is observed in classrooms and elsewhere.					
	g) Planning occurs weekly.					
	h) Data shows that structure contributes to higher levels of student achievement.					
	i) Challenged students have specific behavior plans that work.					
Goal 2	**Indicators**	**A**	**B**	**C**	**D**	**NA**
There is an effective plan for substitutes and volunteers.	a) Handbooks are available.					
	b) Detailed plans and job descriptions are available and followed.					
	c) Staff members know names of substitutes, welcome them, and assist.					
	d) There is evidence of planning and feedback for volunteers.					

Notes:

Checklist # II - Instruction and Learning—Structural Analysis and Assessment						
Goal 3	**Indicators**	**A**	**B**	**C**	**D**	**NA**
There is an effective plan for supervising students in the hallways and restrooms.	a) Staff supervises lines at restrooms effectively.					
	b) Students respond quickly and appropriately to directions from staff.					
	c) Minimal time is wasted moving students from one point to another.					
	d) Movement through hallways is quiet and orderly.					
	e) Organization is evident.					
	f) Little time is wasted between activities.					
	g) Both student attention and behavior at special events are exemplary.					
	h) Adults are actively engaged, moving about instructional areas, and constantly aware of the environment.					
Goal 4	**Indicators**	**A**	**B**	**C**	**D**	**NA**
The reasons for discipline/attitude referrals are minimal.	a) Staff members are empowered to effectively manage students					
	b) Students view all the afterschool staff as authority figures.					
	c) A sense of order, consistency, and cooperation among staff is observable.					
	d) A code of conduct is reinforced.					

Summary Notes:

Identified Norms of Afterschool Program Structure:

Checklist II – Instruction and Learning – Structural Analysis and Assessment

Areas of Strength:

List… (ex. II-1b, etc.)

Targeted Areas for Improvement:

List… (ex. II-2b, etc.)

Adult Behavioral Norms Needed to Achieve Expectations:

Recommendations:

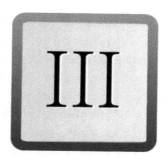

III

Midpoints/Break Time/ Meals & Snacks

Ideas and Advice That Provide Students with Structure and Positive Behaviors When Needed Most

Though no one can go back and make a brand-new start,
anyone can start from now and make a brand-new ending.

\- Anonymous

Introduction

A typical program day may be moving along without incident when suddenly, during snack or meal time, for no apparent reason, everything seems to come unglued. Similarly, after a strong start at the beginning of a year, momentum seems to slow and problems surface more frequently at mid-year. With an uptick of unruly students or disgruntled parents, people search for reasons and rationale for the negativity. Mostly likely, the explanation is that meal time is less-structured and people become lackadaisical after months of routine. When that happens, problems are more likely to occur.

During the transitions from school to the first instructional block and then to snack or meal time, much of the responsibility for supervision of students transfers between adults, sometimes to individuals with varying degrees of responsibility. When those in charge fail to understand the importance of supervision, perform their duties less effectively, or assume that children who are just temporarily under their watch are really another person's problem, cracks in the overall program structure begin to emerge. Students seem to be able to sense these lapses, and typically if you "give them and inch, they will take a mile."

Snack and meal time also signal a break to students. The mid-point of programming can be the time when some parents may begin arriving to pick up their children. Stress increases as adults must multitask. If the receptionist, secretary, or other office staff members fail to be at their stations, some parents, even though they might know better, unabashedly walk right past the sign-out area and proceed to other areas of the program. It only takes one, loose, disgruntled parent in the facility to create an unsafe and chaotic experience for *all* the students and adults.

Effective staffs realize that the play, snack, and mealtime periods are moments when students require heightened levels of supervision and attention. Good planning reduces the potential for trouble. When the adults perform well and effectively supervise students, fewer behavioral problems will require immediate attention and intervention. In addition, the return to the second afternoon instructional block will go much better.

3.1 – Equip Staff for Mid-Program Supervisory Environments

Every staff member should keep a folder or clipboard in a convenient location and carry it with them each time they change their supervisory location. At a minimum, that clipboard should contain:

- a current list of the students to be supervised according to grade and assigned staff member.
- play area rules, guidelines, and supervision expectations.
- site-director referral forms.
- discipline referral forms.
- emergency plans.
- safety gloves.
- pictures of challenging students.

- pictures of any parents (or others) who pose a threat to security.
- pencils, pens, and notepaper.
- paper clips.
- band aids.
- a whistle.
- "Red Card."

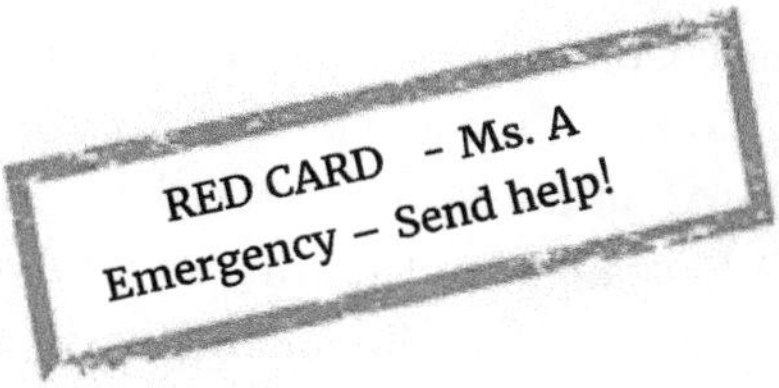

> A "Red Card" includes a staff member's name and a simple message such as:
> *Emergency – send help!*
> *Please alert another adult to inform the office staff and come quickly to assist.*

When aware of a developing crisis, the staff member gives the "Red Card" to a reliable student with instructions to run to find another adult. "Red Cards" are critical forms of communication when time or conditions limit other options.

In the age of technology, adults supervising playgrounds should have access to a reliable system of voice communication with the program office. This might consist of a walkie-talkie, two-way radio, cell phone, or other convenient and reliable form of communication. Be mindful that some two-way radio systems transmit beyond walls and may be monitored by citizens in the surrounding neighborhood.

If allowable in your setting, small digital cameras can be helpful to record and document problems or concerns. Many schools are equipped with cameras. Review your school district and program policies before photographing and releasing pictures of students.

Plan and prepare. It may appear cumbersome for staff to take folders with them to the play or snack area, but planning, training, and proof of preparedness will serve your program stakeholders well in the event of a serious challenge from a disgruntled intruder.

3.2 – Teach Manners & Personal Hygiene

When kids eat, the relative quiet of instructional block can quickly become chaotic. Successful supervision can be sustained throughout the meal and play periods – if the adults don't let down their guard.

At all times, but especially when food is handled, manners and hygiene should be taught and enforced. Structure the rotation of classes through the serving area so that all students have time to use the restroom and wash their hands before they eat. Handwashing with soap and water will help minimize the spread of communicable disease. But children will not always wash without adult reminders. Entire groups of children will skip this routine if they think they can arrive more quickly for snacks and meals.

While waiting in line for food, students should be adequately supervised and taught to remain in their own personal space using inside voices. Students, just as much as adults, should be allowed to talk and socialize. However, children tend to speak louder, especially those from poverty (Payne, 1996). Without structured limits, the noise level in cafeterias will often escalate out of control. All staff in the vicinity of the food service area must share responsibility for teaching and reinforcing appropriate levels of group conversational talk – in a pleasant, respectful manner.

Adults should assure that each child understands appropriate manners in the serving line. Students should be taught to make eye contact, speak in complete sentences with food service staff, and say please and thank you when receiving food. Students will become used to this routine over time, and the positive habits they learn will become part of their behavior when eating out in public restaurants.

3.3 – Facilitate Efficient Food Serving Processes

Many schools are using computerized systems for tracking and maintaining data about students' participation in the lunch program and recording lunch money transactions. Typically, students are given an identification number that can be entered into keypad or a card that can be swiped electronically like a credit transaction. Does your program have access to those systems, or do you utilize something else?

These contemporary systems, sometimes considered too expensive by officials in smaller districts and afterschool programs, likely pay for themselves over a short time by providing better data (which can generate more profit), requiring less time to process individual transactions, providing concerned parents with valuable feedback, and eliminating stigma and easy identification of free or reduced lunch participants in the Federal Lunch Program.

Regardless of how food is served and money is collected (if needed), the processes should be conducted with efficiency. Adequate supervision is necessary. Pleasant midpoint breaks set the tone for the rest of the program day. Teaching and reinforcing structured snack and meal serving processes will help prevent staff from having to deal with improper student interactions the rest of the day. Students become impatient, bored, and misbehave in line when time is wasted in ineffectual processes.

Practice the desired routines of receiving snacks and meals in the serving area. Teach expectations. Conduct refresher sessions throughout the year. Consider the learning needs of the students that join the program at various points throughout the year. All students should learn how to clean, pick up trash around them, and deposit waste.

When adults take the time to teach and model expectations, and stay at it for a period of weeks, everyone will enjoy the positive impact on students' behavior.

3.4 – Consider Play Time First, Eating Afterwards

If you have a play period(s) aligned with snacks and meals, you may want to consider a practice being adopted in many schools – play first, eat afterwards. Research and practice indicate that kids are less rushed when "eat then play" is reversed. The reported positive outcomes include:

- less wasted food – students work up an appetite with exercise.
- students select a better variety of foods.
- fewer digestive concerns – office referrals for upset stomachs drop.
- a more relaxed eating atmosphere.
- fewer conflicts carried into the learning activities after snacks/meals – children return ready to learn.

If this procedure is a change from your current process, it will require planning and time to realize effective results. The physical location of restrooms (for handwashing) and serving areas may present different challenges for student supervision when the schedule is reversed.

Students typically adapt quickly to whatever schedule is established, especially when they receive good training. Resistance to a change in scheduling is more likely to come from adults.

Eat with the children! They are fun to be with and sharing food is a good time to build positive relationships. It is a great time to implement the 2 x 10 relationship-building activity (see Chapter 1, 1.4). When you engage in lively conversation, listen, and learn information that strengthens relationships, the child will leave feeling a special connection with you.

3.5 – Teach Children to Speak with Inside Voices

Young children can learn to speak with inside, *sotto voce* (Italian musical term for *under the voice*) voices. They can learn to distinguish and differentiate the type of vocal volume that is appropriate for physical education classes as well as the library.

Some adults might prefer that children be seen and not heard (as from the adage), but that doesn't help them develop social skills or learn appropriate ways to raise the dozens of questions that they are innately driven to ask. Effective oral communication is essential for an orderly afterschool involvement. When children are taught to temper the loudness of their voices at appropriate times, they are being prepared for numerous middle-class functions. Additionally, adults need to assure that proper eye contact is being made when individuals speak to other people, whether the conversation is initiated by an adult or student.

Most often, children are loud because they are excited and enjoying themselves. However, adults should also recognize that students will be loud when they are modeling what they have observed. Moreover, the voice levels of children will increase most when they are begging for attention.

3.6 – Structure Playground Games

If there is continuous conflict and tension on your playground (created by students, not adults), it may be time to address those issues and develop a plan to achieve better results.

Unfortunately, too many adults dread playground supervision. Some never understand that close observation and a preventative approach of students can eliminate many problems. Others simply grin and bear it, put in their time, complain in the lounge about the students' behavior, and hope for an alternative duty assignment.

If approached differently, with planning focused on students' interests, playground supervision can become a pleasant, refreshing, and relaxing experience for children as well as adults.

Planning Tips

- Assign an adequate number of adults to the playground to assure proper supervision and that the play-space is limited to an area that can always be within view.
- Utilize parent volunteers. There should never be less than two trained adults supervising a playground.
- Develop a schedule of games and activities that students will enjoy. In consideration of students' varying ages, try organizing some of the most common:
  - kickball
  - softball
  - races
  - jump rope
  - hopscotch and four-square
  - cooperative, non-competitive games using parachutes, earth balls, beanbags, balloons etc.
- There should be no limit to what can be scheduled, and a varied weekly schedule will add interest. The point is to simply better organize games and activities and allow students a choice. Work with the students' physical education teacher to reinforce learning objectives from school. Structured, well-supervised play areas have better student engagement, less bullying/fighting, less confusion and debate over rules, fewer excluded students, and hardly any tears. Students can move in and out of games and activities of their choice. To promote healthy exercise habits, all students should be involved in some sort of movement. When they burn off their excess energies, they'll return to the remaining program activities refreshed, relaxed, and ready to learn.

What Would You Do?

Your program is school-based. Midway through the program day, fifth graders are scheduled to have outdoor play time. The boys, especially, enjoy playing basketball. The basketball court is located near the street at the edge of the play area. The rest of the students' favorite play equipment is a considerable distance away and around a corner of the building.

Typically, when the boys play their games, they can become rough. Out-of-control elbows swing causing someone to fall to the ground. When they feel they've been hurt, fifth-grade boys often cry and seek out a supervisory adult. Sometimes, those adults assume the "injury" is the result of a fight. Students involved are sent to the program site-director for intervention.

1. What structures need to be improved?
2. What do adults need to know and be able to do?
3. Where should adults be located?
4. How should "fights" be resolved?
5. How could "fights" be prevented?

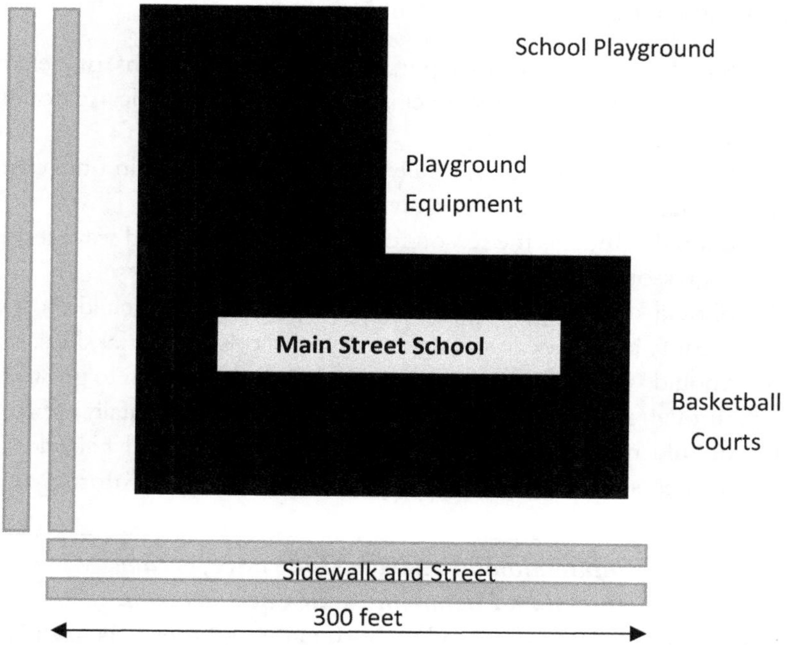

3.7 – Teach Adults How to Prevent Bullying

At any age, bullying is defined as any physical action or verbal behavior intended to cause fear towards someone who has less social or physical power. Bullying spreads in schools and afterschool programs when adults fail to recognize or acknowledge power gaps between children. Hurtful behaviors that adults may brush off as insignificant can become a pattern of bullying, especially when they are repeated, intense, and targeted.

Among school-age children and youth, bullying stems from immature social-emotional development and relationship-building skills. Acting in hurtful ways fulfills a need for attention and/or control. To prevent bullying, adults must intervene by defining what behaviors are hurtful, set limits, and problem-solve with students to help facilitate the development of positive relationships.

A child or adult becomes a bully when they repeat manipulative behaviors over and over to gain some sort of egocentric power and satisfaction. Aggressive bullying erodes a program culture by expanding levels of anxiety and fear, escalating toxic feelings, and increasing intimidation to destructive levels.

What Adults Should and Should Not Do

1. Should - Recognize that purposeful, hurtful patterns of behavior are signs that a child is experiencing difficulties with physical, emotional, and social development.
2. Should not - Isolate the "bully" with a consequence in time-out, as that will likely escalate their negative behavior.
3. Should - Address the reason for the behavior and find ways for both the aggressor and victim(s) to express their feelings.
4. Should - Seize opportunities to help and support all children and youth identify constructive strategies to express positive social skills.
5. Should - Teach, intervene, support, and allow children to grow and work through situations themselves as may be developmentally appropriate.
6. Should not - Ignore patterns of purposeful, hurtful behavior. Report incidents of bullying. Seek support from colleagues. Inform parents.

***Unintentional* behavior, done once, is *rude*.**
***Intentional* behavior, done once, is *mean*.**
***Repeated intentional* behavior, both rude and mean, is *bullying*.**

Planning Tips

1. School districts must use the same language within all its schools in order to reduce bullying. Confirm that your program's definition is aligned with your school district and explained in your student-parent handbook. Assure that your staff is familiar with state and federal laws that pertain to bullying.
2. Teach staff members their responsibility to report student-to-student child abuse should it develop.
3. Set clear, consistent, and enforceable expectations in a code of conduct.
4. Assure that staff members are visible and effectively supervising their students' interactions during times of transition and other hot spots. Identify where and when those challenging times of the day are most likely to be. Teach staff to identify warning signs. Not all negative behavior leads to bullying.
5. Build rapport and relationships during transitions. Positive conversations reduce chances of hurtful behavior. When students (and adults) feel a connection, they will be more likely to talk openly about their problem, thus reducing the incidence of bullying.
6. Avoid labeling children as bullies. Instead, address the behaviors that are hurtful and enable the child to learn and grow. Reward positive behavior.
7. Develop a plan for informing parents about bullying. Communication with parents about bullying can be tricky. Having established a good rapport helps when it becomes time to discuss concerns, whether their child is a perpetrator or on the receiving end of bullying behavior.
8. Bullies love an audience. Remove those involved in conflict from others.
9. Institute bullying prevention activities such as anti-bullying assemblies, positive communications campaigns, and creative arts contests highlighting program values that bring people together and reinforce the message that bullying is wrong.
10. To effectively eliminate bullying by children, assure that bullying by adults does not exist anywhere in your program.

How to Manage "That Kid"

Many afterschool professionals feel like their students are out of control at one time or another. But usually, that feeling doesn't last long. Yet, in some cases, and with *that kid*, out-of-control becomes the norm. *That kid* always seems to be the one who refuses to listen, breaks the rules, and couldn't care less about any consequences.

Most kids like rules and limits. They feel safe in programs where they trust adults who set and enforce rules. When they lack that trust, they experience a lot of distress and anxiety. Anguish, no matter its source, leads to increased incidence of behavior problems. It is often a cause of defiance and fighting.

To help *that kid* become successful, try these dozen strategies:

1. Check-in before triggers develop. (see Chapter 1, 1.4, The 2x10 Relationship Builder)
2. Build a relationship. Too much pressure, and the relationship with *that kid* can be squashed. Not enough, and *that kid* gets away from you.
3. Maintain proximity while supervising cautiously. *That kid* may need time and space.
4. Reward effort in unique ways. *That kid* is unique and likely won't respond to rewards that others value.
5. Teach wait time. Help *that kid* overcome the need for self-gratification.
6. Develop "in between" steps in transitions.
7. Provide biofeedback tools. Many defiant kids need pictures and other tools and reminders to help identify de-escalation strategies.
8. Give a child a "preview" of work. *That kid* very well might respond better in class if given a preview of the lesson and a question to answer correctly before the lesson is taught.
9. Teach persistence skills. (Read ahead to Chapter 4, 4.4)
10. Teach alternative responses to confrontations. (See 3.14 in this chapter)
11. Assign leadership responsibility. Given some positive attention and praise, *that kid* is likely to respond in positive ways.
12. Initiate random acts of kindness. Implement this strategy throughout the program.

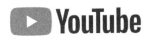

As a staff, watch *Three Letters from Teddy*
https://youtu.be/xVzvg6hiF0g YouTube

3.8 – Establish Procedures for Indoor Play Activities

When it rains, snows, or the weather is unfit to allow outdoor play, plan for indoor play activities. Without a structural plan and specific guidelines and attention to supervision, indoor play periods can present numerous concerns and problems, quickly becoming the most at-risk period of the program day. It is important that supervisory expectations for indoor and outdoor play periods become well-known and established.

Planning Tips

- Teach expectations. Kids need to know their parameters. Let them know what they can play with, where, with whom, and how loud their voices should be.
- Assign seating and play areas. Some kids will be more physical than others. Proactively make specific seating assignments and structure play areas for challenged students before they leave the play area.
- Provide children with a variety of games, exploratory and enrichment center-based activities, and computer programs that engage students while reinforcing academic skills. Other ideas to effectively occupy time might include:
    - ➢ educational videos and DVDs (combine classes for easier supervision).
    - ➢ board games (checkers, chess, etc.) that can be played individually, as couples, or in small groups.
    - ➢ drawing and arts and crafts activities.
    - ➢ computer access.
    - ➢ blackboard games.
    - ➢ cooperative games.
    - ➢ pre-arranged visits and access to the school library or music room.
    - ➢ storytelling conducted by volunteers.
    - ➢ private sustained reading opportunities.
    - ➢ seat and floor exercises.
- There is no limit to what can be imagined, planned, and implemented. Where there is good planning and expectations are continuously reinforced, problems are minimized.

3.9 – Take Pictures and Use Recorders

During program registration, permission and authorization should be obtained from a child's parent or guardian for a variety of special events and activities: bus field trips, walking field trips, internet access, and identification and inclusion of students in yearbooks, photographs, publications, websites, etc. Know your policies and follow them. Align them with students' schools. Inform parents if there are security cameras that will capture students' actions in the school, the afterschool program, play area, and any buses that might be used.

Take pictures. They will help tell your story in a variety of formats. Invest and utilize technologies that support afterschool structure and student management.

Develop a policy for student and adult usage of cell phones during the program time. Most cell phones come equipped with cameras. Their usage can be positive and negative. They can disrupt classes. They can also be valuable learning tools and a convenient means to collect photos. They can be misplaced or stolen. Regardless, cell phones are prevalent, and effective policies are needed to assure their presence is positive.

Many boards of education have developed policies (often accessible on-line) that permit video security cameras to be used on school buses and playgrounds. The policies, and the rationale behind them, likely are varied, but they generally are designed for the purpose of improving student discipline and assuring the health, safety, and welfare of everyone. Every program staff must continuously consider what is needed to assure student welfare. It is prudent to collaboratively develop administrative policies that clarify the widespread utilization of cameras, recording devices, and cellular communication technologies. Make sure that all laws, regulations, and policies allow such practices and that parents and other stakeholders are informed of the program's plans.

3.10 – Establish Contingency Plans for Crisis Supervision

Planning for every type of problem or emergency that might occur is an enormous responsibility. Every staff member must be aware of several predetermined safe havens where they should calmly relocate students in the event of an extended building evacuation. They must also have plans for supervising students and communicating with parents and each other during unforeseen, stressful situations.

If a student or staff member suddenly becomes ill, does everyone know what to do and how to respond? How about a power outage? An intruder? The list of concerns and subsequent contingencies can be endless. Programs are most at risk during transition periods and dismissals.

Schools must file safety plans with state regulatory agencies. Get a copy and make sure your program policies and practice align. Make sure all adults know and are properly trained to follow the plans.

Again, cell phones can provide immediate access to help during emergencies. They also provide immediate access to parents – and parent access to their kids. Forms of access should be addressed as part of your security plan.

3.11 – Teach Children to Speak in Complete Sentences

The middle part of the program day is an ideal time for adults to engage students in conversations, model appropriate speaking skills, and insist that skills learned in the classroom are practiced in freedom of social settings, especially when playing and eating . What are some of the benefits?

- <u>Reinforcement of correct grammar</u>. The child will hear and learn that it is incorrect to say, for example, "That boy *don't* like pizza!" or "Billy *had went* to the wrong door." The ability to self-correct can have a direct correlation to higher test scores when that same child must read a story and select right answers from distracters.
- <u>Reinforcement of the skills taught in language arts classes</u> related to the identification and usage of nouns, verbs, adjectives and adverbs.
- <u>Expansion of vocabulary</u>. Students of poverty are less likely to know and use as many words as their peers (Payne, 1996). Speaking in complete sentences helps the teacher and child focus, practice, and improve language usage together.
- <u>Better oral and aural skills</u>. While listening, the teacher must encourage proper eye contact, vocal volume and inflections, and other nuances of speech. Children also become better accustomed to speaking to adults and each other.

Musicians know that the ability to perform lyrical phrases correctly, to make aural sense, and convey the composer's deep meaning and message, requires extensive practice. So does learning to speak a language.

So why consider this tip? It is a sound strategy that enriches student-teacher interactions. It reinforces language instruction during times of the day where formal learning may not be the primary focus. Speaking in complete sentences, when modeled and consistently reinforced throughout a school from the beginning of the day to the end (and start of year to the end), can contribute to higher test scores. Where the structure is such that every adult expects and helps students learn to speak in complete sentences, appropriate use of language improves. It requires effort and commitment from all adults. It works!

3.12 – Help Children Gain the Verbal Advantage

Every child must learn to respond to a teacher's question, give an oral report, speak on the phone, participate in a job interview, or converse with adults in social settings. The ability to speak effectively in public provides listeners with an immediate impression of the interviewee's background and educational level. Being poised and able to speak effectively can sometimes be more important than the ability to pass a written test.

The world's best leaders are great orators. They learn not only what to say, but how to say it well – accurately and with confidence. To become leaders of their generation, young learners must gain an oral advantage

Parents are the first to teach their child to talk. The first words are a memorable time in a child's development. That development must continue for a lifetime as an individual works for mastery of the oral advantage. The formative years in school are critical for later maturity. Parents must be involved and work closely with school officials, establish high expectations, model correct forms of speaking, and listen. Children who achieve the oral advantage will reap rewards in a multitude of ways throughout their adult lives. That is a magnanimous gift to give to children.

Verbal Advantage Planning Tips

- Insist that children speak in complete sentences. Starting sentences with "because" or answering questions with a shoulder shrug does not help students gain an advantage. Utilize a signal that reminds them that must self-correct. A unified effort will help all children and adults.
- Model appropriate speaking skills. At school, students must learn and practice the formal vs. casual registers of written and oral language. Develop innovative questions that will become conversation starters.
- Build vocabulary – Reading teachers have lists of basic words that all children should recognize and understand for success in each grade. Help children relate them to learning experiences outside school.
- Make eye contact when speaking. Mumbling or avoiding eye contact can lead to negative first impressions.
- Use correct grammar. Young children who learn to say "It don't get any better than this" will find "It doesn't get any better than this" to appear strange on standardized reading tests.
- Avoid slang, colloquialisms, unnecessary sounds and incomplete words. Using slang inappropriately can become embarrassing. Model how to finish suffixes (ex. "going vs. gonna" "reading vs. readin'). Interviewers rate those who muddy their thoughts with numerous "you knows" or "uhs" lower than those who speak correctly.
- Avoid bad habits. Students who can't structure a sentence without using the word "like" demonstrate immature language development.
- Teach the importance of pronunciations, volume, and tempo. Mispronounce words, and likely children will as well.
- Seek professional help early. Consult with school officials for persistent pronunciation problems.
- Encourage your students to speak in public. Encourage children to participate in plays at school and church, to memorize poems and stories, to talk at the dinner table, and to take advantage of talk-time in the car. Model public speaking for children and listen.
- Encourage parents to monitor the TV. Parents should turn it off if the language is incorrect or inappropriate. Television, without controls, can be the source of many bad oral habits.

Common Mispronounced Words and Phrases

	Don't say…	***Do say…***
1.	acrossed	across
2.	ath*e*lete or ath*e*letic	ath-lete, ath-let-ic
3.	chester drawers	chest of drawers
4.	di*a*late	dilate
5.	drownd	drown
6.	e*x*cape	e*s*cape
7.	ex-cetera	et cetera
8.	Feb*you*ary	Feb*ru*ary
9.	heigh*th*	heigh*t*
10.	inter*pretate*	inter*pret*
11.	*ir*regardless	regardless
12.	jew*lery*	*jewel*ry
13.	libary	lib*ra*ry
14.	mannaise	*may*onnaise
15.	miniture	mini*a*ture
16.	'nother	another
17.	nuc*u*lar	nucl*e*ar
18.	orientate	orient
19.	*per*scription	*pre*scription
20.	*pre*spire	*per*spire
21.	prob*ly*	prob-ab-ly
22.	pro*noun*ciation	pro*nun*ciation
23.	sherbe*r*t	sher*bet*
24.	snuck	sneaked
25.	stomp out	stamp out
26.	suppos*ab*ly	suppos*ed*ly
27.	tri-ath-a-lon	tri-ath-lon
28.	u*p*most	u*t*most
29.	ver-*bage*	verb-i-age
30.	wa*d*n't	wa*s*n't

3.13 – Invite Guests to Observe

When you invite guests to your home, you clean up, dress up, and put your best self forward. The same should happen when you invite guests to your afterschool program. Kids should be informed of visits of impending guests, reminded of the positive behaviors they should exhibit, and encouraged to use their vocal skills to make good impressions. When students receive compliments, which most adults need no reminding to offer, praise typically encourages even higher levels of positive behavior.

We all have a choice. We can purposefully and proactively create environments where students' positive behaviors feed self-confidence and create additional pleasurable experiences, or we can react to negativity and all the stress associated with it. Involving and including everyone in the preparatory and anticipatory activities of hosting guests encompasses many positive interactions. Try it. Enjoy the benefits.

Try this activity (shared with permission of Ms. Danielle Dunkel (@MissDunkel), Ohio University Graduate 2018, see Figures 3.13a, 3.13b, and 3.13c).

Over a period of weeks or months of program activities, have students keep a portfolio of their work. As a culminating activity, invite guests from the community to visit and conduct conversations (or mock interviews) with the students as they show their portfolios and respond to impromptu questions the guest might ask. Besides what the students must do to create the portfolio, their preparatory work would involve improving public speaking, eye contact, body language, etc. – all the soft skills that social psychologists are identifying as being as important to success in school and the workplace as cognitive abilities – maybe even more important. Invite anyone in your community who would help and be a role model for the kids (mayor, business people, clergy, political figures, teachers, administrators, older students, etc.)

Schedule interview rounds of 10-15 minutes. Students show their portfolio to the interviewee. Those waiting for their turn could observe their peers being interviewed, or the interviews could take place in another room. The materials that follow could be modified to fit your specific needs and goals. Be sure to allot time for the guests to provide positive feedback to students. This will become a peak moment in the students' experience with your program.

Figure 3.13a

The Mock Interview

Note to Community Members: The interviews you are asked to conduct are a culminating activity of students' academic work and achievement in our afterschool program. Our goals for them in this activity are:

a) a good first-impression (manners, smile, eye contact, posture, body language)
b) demonstrate organizational skills (well-presented portfolio of work)
c) effective speaking skills (good grammar, no "like" or "um" – no verbal graffiti)
d) strengthening sense of self-concept
e) vocalization of personal goals
f) preparation for work and success in the real world.

Below are questions you may use to guide the students through the interviews. You do not have to ask all these questions. Pick a few questions and allow the interview to unfold naturally. Please note, many of these students have never experienced this kind of activity before. For some, this might be their first time sitting down with a successful community leader and talking. Please, have patience, kindness and fun with these students. There will be two rounds, which are attached on the next page. There is a rubric provided to give them feedback. Thank you for your time!

Icebreaker Questions:

- What do you enjoy most about school and the afterschool program?
- What do you enjoy doing when you are at home?
- What is your favorite part of the school day?
- What is your least favorite part of the school day?
- What do you like most about the afterschool program?
- What is your favorite subject? What do you like about it?

Questions about Portfolios:

- Describe something challenging you have overcome.
- Explain one of your greatest moments in the afterschool program.
- Based on what you've learned compiling this portfolio, what would be your plan for making your work better?

Questions about Goals:

- What goals have you developed because of this interview?
- What are your goals for the rest of the school year? Explain how you plan on accomplishing these goals.
- What kind of a career do you hope to pursue when older?

Questions about the Future:

- What are your hopes for (middle school; high school; ____________?
- What do you want people to think and say about you at your school?
- Who would you most want to like?
- Who do you most admire in the world and why?

Figure 3.13.b

Interview Rubric

Criteria	4: Excellent	3: Acceptable	2: Good	1: Needs Work
Introduction	Greeting Handshake Manners Eye Contact Body Language Ability to Click	Greeting Handshake Manners Eye Contact Body Language Ability to Click	Greeting Handshake Manners Eye Contact Body Language Ability to Click	Greeting Handshake Manners Eye Contact Body Language Ability to Click
Presentation (Appearance, Expression, Voice)	Posture Eye Contact Body Language Confidence Expressiveness Grammar No Verbal Graffiti No Bad Habits Good Impression	Posture Eye Contact Body Language Confidence Expressiveness Grammar No Verbal Graffiti No Bad Habits Good Impression	Posture Eye Contact Body Language Confidence Expressiveness Grammar No Verbal Graffiti No Bad Habits Good Impression	Posture Eye Contact Body Language Confidence Expressiveness Grammar No Verbal Graffiti No Bad Habits Good Impression
Preparation	Knowledgeable Confident Pride Progress Evident	Knowledgeable Confident Pride Progress Evident	Knowledgeable Confident Pride Progress Evident	Knowledgeable Confident Pride Progress Evident
Responses to Questions From Interviewer	Awareness Good Fluency Eye Contact Focused Competence Explanations	Awareness Good Fluency Eye Contact Focused Competence Explanations	Awareness Good Fluency Eye Contact Focused Competence Explanations	Awareness Good Fluency Eye Contact Focused Competence Explanations
Questions asked by Interviewee	Shows Interest Insightful Pertinent Practical Commonsense Expressive	Shows Interest Insightful Pertinent Practical Commonsense Expressive	Shows Interest Insightful Pertinent Practical Commonsense Expressive	Shows Interest Insightful Pertinent Practical Commonsense Expressive

Figure 3.13c

Interview Rounds

Round I (Time - Time)

Round	Ms. A	Mr. B	Ms. C	Mr. D	Ms. E
1	*Student 1*	*Student 4*	*Student 7*	*Student 10*	*Student 13*
2	*Student 2*	*Student 5*	*Student 8*	*Student 11*	*Student 14*
3	*Student 3*	*Student 6*	*Student 9*	*Student 12*	*Student 15*

Round II (Time - Time)

Round	Ms. A	Mr. B	Ms. C	Mr. D	Ms. E
1	*Student 16*	*Student 19*	*Student 22*	*Student 25*	*Student 28*
2	*Student 17*	*Student 20*	*Student 23*	*Student 26*	*Student 29*
3	*Student 18*	*Student 21*	*Student 24*	*Student 27*	*Student 30*

- Figure 3.13a, 3.13b, and 3.13c shared with permission of @MissDunkel

3.14 – Develop a Conflict Mediation Program

Inevitably, conflicts develop. Disagreements typically start because of lack of attention, differing interests, weak interpersonal skills, and developmental immaturity. Many people assume conflict is bad, but not always. Kids need to experience conflict and learn to cope using social skills that are appropriate in society. Moms and dads must learn that there are times they should not interfere and let kids learn to solve their own problems. Everyone benefits from learning about the causes of conflict and resolution strategies. Conflict management programs provide students with a sense of self-empowerment.

Unfortunately, many effective conflict management programs fade away when adults become preoccupied with other activities or lose interest. Student conflict management programs require adult supervision and facilitation. For long term success, a staff must be committed to planning, reflection, evaluation, and continuous improvement.

Planning Tips

- Consult with your local mental health agencies or social workers for help in acquiring materials and instructional guides for starting conflict or peer mediation programs. Court officials also have resources they can share.
- Invite trained personnel that can provide special programs or consult with school staff and empower them to deliver instruction.
- Talk with colleagues in other schools for their recommendations for conflict mediate program.
- The Internet contains innumerable sites related to the topic, such as:
    - http://www.njsbf.com/njsbf/student/conflictres/elementary.cfm New Jersey State Bar Foundation
    - http://www.indiana.edu/~safeschl/resources_mediation.html - Indiana University
    - http://www.ianrpubs.unl.edu/epublic/pages/publicationD.jsp?publicationId=147 – University of Nebraska
    - http://www.violencepreventionweek.org/index.html?menu=resources&l=3 National Youth Violence Prevention Campaign

3.15 – Share Successes with the School Principal

For your afterschool program to be successful, recognition and support from the school principal is essential. Principals are busy people. They love good news. They can leverage staff, resources, space, time, and much more for your program if they are well-informed and view the program positively. Invite them to observe the program frequently. Showcase the positive behaviors students display and the progress they make.

What principal wouldn't make time to visit if she received a special invitation from a student?

Despite very busy and often hectic schedules, principals will agree to meet and plan, learn about progress, discuss concerns, and leverage support if they view the program site-director as an ally, a problem solver and solution provider rather than a source of problems and negativity. If you request a weekly, standing, twenty-minute meeting with him, you'll likely get it. See Figure 3.14 for a sample agenda which can easily be developed in a table format using a word processing program. Resize and modify it to meet your needs. Once the meeting concept and date have been agreed upon, email the agenda to the principal a day in advance, and follow-up with your notes soon afterward. The principal will love that she doesn't have to prepare the paperwork. Your professionalism will impress. Show flexibility and understanding when your meeting gets bumped due to an emergency.

Visit the **After School and Summer Learning Portal**
of The National Association of Elementary Principals (NAESP)
for resources and information that will support and strengthen the
alignment of your program with that of your students' school(s).
http://afterschool.naesp.org
naesp

Figure 3.14

The Twenty Minute Meeting

Main Street Elementary School
Main Street Community Learning Center
Any Town, USA

AGENDA

Weekly Collaborative Planning Meeting
Tuesday, 10:00 a. m.
Day, Month, Year

Time	Topic	Person who will prepare and lead discussion	Discuss/Decide/ Delegate	Desired Outcomes	Notes *(complete after meeting)*
10:00	Johnny J., Gr. 2; *Reading challenges*	Site-Director	Discuss; Determine interventions for afterschool program	Reading performance on grade level	
10:08	Susie M. *Homework difficulties*	Site-Director	Principal requested to get information from teacher	Less stress; higher % of completion; more appropriate assignments	
10:15	What works?	Principal	Discuss program vision	Clarity of direction	
10:17	Areas for improving?	Site-Director	Turf issues with community sports groups	Shared space, resources	
10:19	Next meeting	Site-Director	plan	List agenda/topic ideas	
10:20	End		summarize	summarize	Who? How are notes shared and maintained?

Summary

If you ask young children to identify what they like most about school, a popular response will be "lunch and recess!" In contrast, adults may choose lunch as a favorite time, but they are less likely to include recess with that same answer.

How we speak (the sound, tone, dynamics, contrasts, accuracy, etc.) contributes to an attitude of positivity. Assure that improving and sustaining positive verbal communication is a focus of your work. However, every musician knows that effective non-verbal communication is just as essential. Can you communicate important messages using your eyes and hands? Are non-verbal communication techniques used consistently? See Appendix 6 for some ideas.

Staffs that perform at the master level understand the pitfalls of supervision and student management that detract from a smooth, organized program operation. They focus on teaching expectations, prevention instead of reaction, positive attitudes instead of negativity, and shared responsibility for school and afterschool success. They avoid the common avoidance syndrome found in many educational settings. Adults say, "Let me help" rather than "That's not my responsibility right now."

Without a doubt, there are many other midday and midyear issues that will be unique to various program sizes and locations that require adult attention. This chapter is intended to be a springboard for helping the reader focus and identify those situations and determine strategies for increased effectiveness. This kind of planning makes for a pleasant and satisfying midday or midyear experience for everyone.

Checklist III—Midpoints/Break Time/Meals & Snacks—Structural Analysis and Assessment

Goal 1	Indicators	A	B	C	D	NA
The environment is efficient, orderly, and enjoyable.	a) Teachers and program assistants effectively supervise students in lines and while eating					
	b) Students observe rules of good manners and hygiene.					
	c) Student behavioral problems are minimal.					
	d) "Cafeteria" inside voices are appropriate.					
	e) There are positive results from the implementation of a code of conduct.					
	f) Technology is evident that supports efficacy.					
	g) Students eat balanced, nutritious snacks and meals.					

Goal 2	Indicators	A	B	C	D	NA
There is an effective plan for moving students from the eating areas to and from instructional areas, the playground, or elsewhere.	a) Attention is paid to forming lines					
	b) Safety is always observed .					
	c) There is evidence of planning and input from all staff.					
	d) Staff behavioral norms are observed.					
	Notes:					

Goal 3	Indicators	A	B	C	D	NA
There is an effective supervisory plan for students during outdoor or indoor play times.	a) Varied communication needs are addressed					
	b) Emergency planning is evident.					
	c) A variety of activities for students is planned.					
	d) Minimal time is wasted moving students from one point to another.					
	e) Movement through hallways is quiet and orderly.					

Checklist III—Midpoints/Break Time/Meals & Snacks—Structural Analysis and Assessment						
Goal 3	**Indicators**	**A**	**B**	**C**	**D**	**NA**
	a) Organization is evident.					
	b) Little time is wasted between instruction and other activities.					
	c) All staff members maintain interaction using positive voices with students during snacks, meals serving, eating areas, and elsewhere.					
Goal 4	**Indicators**	**A**	**B**	**C**	**D**	**NA**
Staff interacts and communicates with students and parents in a positive manner.	a) Parents are greeted with eye contacts, smiles, and courtesy.					
	b) A code of conduct is reinforced.					
	c) Students and adults speak in complete sentences.					
	d) Conflict is acknowledged and resolved peacefully.					
	e) A sense of order, consistency, and cooperation among staff is observable.					

Summary Notes:

Identified Norms of Afterschool Program Structure:

Checklist III—Midpoints/Break Time/Meals & Snacks—Structural Analysis and Assessment

Areas of Strength:

List… (ex. III-1b, etc.)

Targeted Areas for Improvement:

List… (ex. III-2b, etc.)

Adult Behavioral Norms Needed to Achieve Expectations:

Recommendations:

IV

Second Half (After 5:00 p.m.)

Ideas and Advice That Provide Positive Outcomes for Learners of All Ages

Introduction

Students typically have the ability and rigor to do whatever adults request. One concern that permeates the regular school day, as well as afterschool, is that adults gradually become tired, show less enthusiasm, and let down their guard the longer they work. They start strong and finish weak. They become negative.

Similar concerns appear during the slumps, humps, and stressful periods of midyear. Sustaining work with vigor and enthusiasm can be challenging. The series of topics discussed in this chapter, and others that readers are encouraged to brainstorm and identify for their afterschool programs, are presented to provide ideas and advice that support positive developments during the challenging later times of the day and year.

4.1 – Reading Is Always a Positive Learning Activity

With rising concern about how much screen time kids have with various electronic devices, reading books is an activity that is generally thought to be beneficial. But creating fun and positive reading activities can involve more than books. Consider developing a variety of reading challenges for students that remain in your program before their pick-up time. In addition to books, encourage kids to find ways to expand reading of everything pertaining to their interest and environment.

Reading is an activity everyone should support. Kids will mimic what they see adults do and what they hear them say. Kids develop a love of reading from influential adults.

Develop simple motivational games that encourage greater amounts of times spent reading. Get a clear plastic jar and label it as shown in Figure 4.1. Allow students to fill it with marbles, beans, or even candy and celebrate accordingly when it fills and reaches various lines.

Figure 4.1

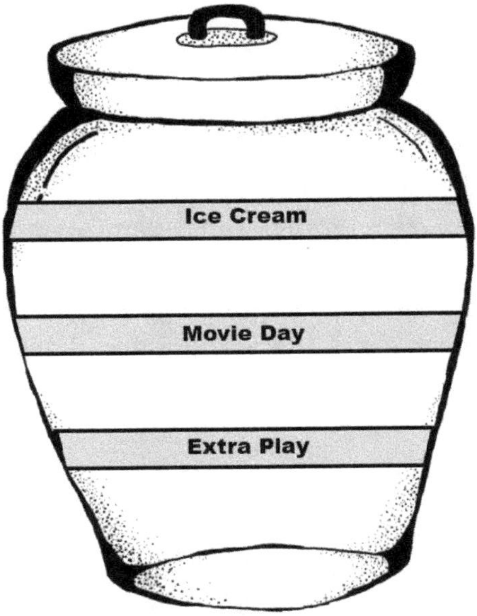

4.2 – Write Personal Notes and Make Positive Phone Calls

There is never very much "down" time in a well-structured program day. Many essential activities need to be integrated in order to accomplish goals. Two aspirations – the development of written and oral language – can be reinforced and advanced by teaching kids how to write personal notes and make positive phone calls.

Every good mentor instills these habits in their protégé. The act of writing a personal thank you or congratulatory note demonstrates that you sincerely want to show gratitude, acknowledgement, or recognition for another's acts. Set a personal goal to write three of them each day.

Planning Tips

- Create some simple, inexpensive note cards as seen in Figure 4.2.
- Brainstorm with students lists of people to whom they could write personal notes (parents, siblings, relatives, teachers, friends, volunteers, etc.)
- Discuss types of note messages (thank you, congratulatory, encouragement, etc.)
- Staff can assist to assure that notes are delivered effectively (ex. - those to school personnel could be collected and delivered to the school.

Figure 4.2

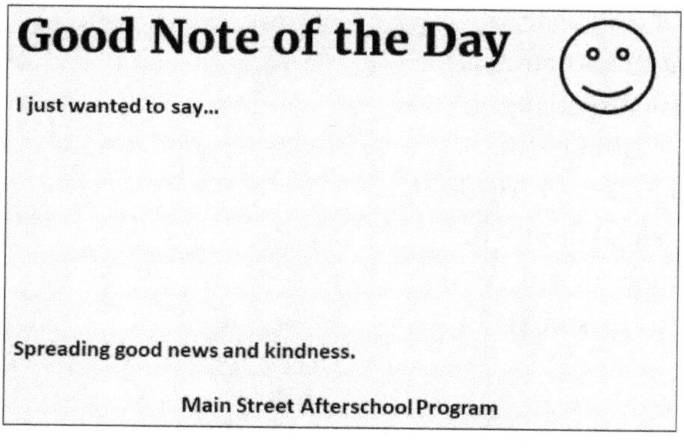
Good Note of the Day

I just wanted to say...

Spreading good news and kindness.

Main Street Afterschool Program

A popular practice of many school administrators is called "Good News Call of the Day."[8] Develop your recognition criteria and allow the student to make a call to their parent with the program site-director. Follow-up with a tweet or other form of social media recognition. The positive return on time invested will be worth it. And if by chance you get an answering machine, ask to be called back. Everyone likes good news. And then, if you have a negative to convey to a parent, it is always easier for them to receive.

The habit of writing notes of appreciation and making upbeat phones calls will produce many positive behaviors. Adults should emulate what they teach.

4.3 – Teach Multiple Intelligences

Do you have some students who find it difficult to sit still? They want to tap and pound on anything around them. They may grow up to become drummers in the school band. If you understand the theory of multiple intelligences and create learning experiences that help develop them, you'll increase positive experiences for many of your students. The theory of multiple intelligences helps explain why many kids are so talented manipulating their bodies, others so quick to recognize words, or still others to grasp complex mathematics concepts.

The concept that humans possessed intelligences in non-traditional was first proposed by developmental psychologist Howard Gardner in his 1983 book *Frames of Mind: The Theory of Multiple Intelligences.* Originally, he identified seven forms of intelligence:

1. musical-rhythmic.
2. visual-spatial.
3. verbal-linguistic.
4. logical-mathematical.
5. bodily-kinesthetic.
6. interpersonal.
7. intrapersonal.

[8] Check out #goodnewscalloftheday on Twitter.

He later suggested that existential and moral intelligences may also be worthy of inclusion.

Multiple intelligences should be addressed at all hours of the day, but staff and students may enjoy a special daily focus on one or more during the time before pick-up. Work with your students' school teachers to align and extend activities related to:

- Linguistic intelligence: a sensitivity to the meaning and order of words.
- Logical-mathematical intelligence: ability in mathematics and other complex logical systems.
- Musical intelligence: the ability to understand and create music. Musicians, composers and dancers show a heightened musical intelligence.
- Spatial intelligence: the ability to "think in pictures," to perceive the visual world accurately, and recreate (or alter) it in the mind or on paper. Spatial intelligence is highly developed in artists, architects, designers and sculptors.
- Bodily-kinesthetic intelligence: the ability to use one's body in a skilled way, for self-expression or toward a goal. Mimes, dancers, basketball players, and actors are among those who display bodily-kinesthetic intelligence.
- Interpersonal intelligence: an ability to perceive and understand other individuals – their moods, desires, and motivations. Political and religious leaders, skilled parents and teachers, and therapists use this intelligence.
- Intrapersonal intelligence: an understanding of one's own emotions. Some novelists and or counselors use their own experience to guide others.
- Naturalist intelligence: an ability to recognize and classify plants, minerals, and animals, including rocks and grass and all variety of flora and fauna.

4.4 – Teach the Concepts of Grit and Mindset

Many students lack the ability to stick with assignments or projects when they are hard or require focused attention and time to complete. They throw up their hands and quit. Their frustration leads to negative behaviors.

There is extensive research on the topic of social-emotional learning. Many schools are designing special programs and adding specialists to help develop these skills. Some forms of standardized measurement of students' skills are also emerging. Consult with your students' school(s) to align your work and expand on their efforts.

Written especially for afterschool professionals, check out my book *Teaching Grit and Mindset in Afterschool Programs: What students, staff, and parents should know and be able to do*. It is an easy-to-use, hands-on guide for understanding and teaching the success skills – grit and mindset – in the afterschool program environment. If you are working with kids who have potential but don't want to do anything, you'll benefit from the book's quick staff development ideas and reflective exercises. Together, we can teach kids how to increase their perseverance and develop the growth mindset traits and motivation to complete homework and be fully engaged in out-of-school learning.

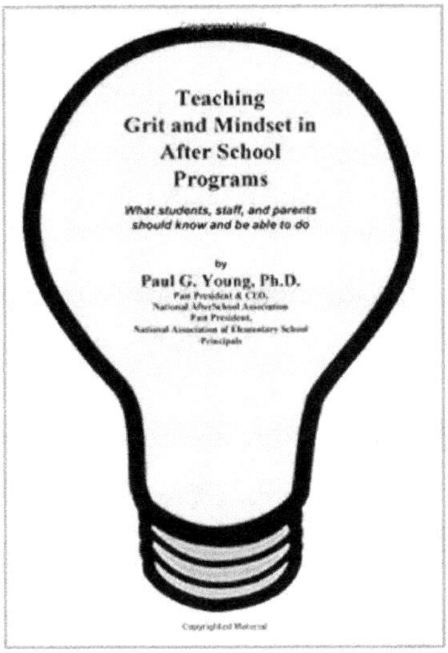

Available from Amazon.com

Dealing with Apathy

Who is responsible for the child who appears not to care and doesn't want to do anything? You've likely heard that when a student can't learn the way you teach, you should teach the way that the student learns. That thinking has led us to the point where too many kids think that if a lesson, assignment, or a class fails to interest them, they don't have to care about it. If lessons fail to be interactive like the video games they love, they become inattentive. Teachers are expected to entertain, to make all learning fun and games.

That can wear you down, and it doesn't prepare kids for the real world.

Kids (and adults) must learn to take responsibility for their learning. Unfortunately, there isn't a "program" that can easily be implemented to reverse the learned bad habits that have led to a state of apathy. While delivering instruction in the most engaging manner possible, adults must reverse those habits by teaching the importance of organization, perseverance, and hard work. That requires a personal relationship with a child and a commitment to change bad habits in small steps. Focus on teaching and strengthening common work-ethic skills such as:

Attitude – effective body language, eye contact, smile, and enthusiasm.

Commonsense – intelligent thinking and decision-making in everyday situations that helps students avoid irrational mistakes.

Gratitude – is an attitude of manners, etiquette, and appreciation.

Initiative – one of the most sought-after skills by employers. Teach kids to ask at least one question each day.

Integrity – no matter what, kids must learn to tell the truth and do the right thing. Teach them to do what they say they will do when they say they will do it. Be sure to model that mantra.

Persistence (grit) – never give up. Teach kids to finish what they start.

Reliability – dependable, punctual, accurate, responsible, and trustworthy.

Respectful – teach kids to show they care and value other perspectives.

Teaching routine lessons while incorporating the values associated with a good work-ethic benefits all children – especially those needing to improve motivation. Start small. Build a relationship. Focus on changing the mindset. Celebrate small victories. Success breeds success, and success is an excellent motivator.

The Benefits of Extracurricular Activities

Extracurricular activities are typically outside the realm of the normal school curriculum.

It should be no surprise that students who participate in extracurricular activities, especially in high school, are better prepared for success in the workforce or post-secondary studies than those who do not. In fact, Angela Duckworth, in her book *Grit: The Power of Passion and Perseverance*, stated that:

> If I could wave a magic wand, I'd have all the children in the world engage in at least one extracurricular activity of their choice, and as for those in high school, I'd require that they stick with at least one activity for more than a year.[9]

Among the benefits of being coached, other advantages include opportunities to build relationships, a reduction in behavioral issues, better time-management, higher grades, increased self-esteem – all antidotes for apathy.

Unfortunately, Duckworth and other researchers note that demographics, such as socio-economic background, create numerous challenges with negative impacts on students' access to popular extracurricular opportunities, especially those from poorer areas. But where those challenges exist, afterschool programs can help.

Students need to begin participation in many activities at an early age. Creative thinking, planning, and strategies can help students overcome costs of participation, supplies, transportation, pay-to-play fees, and many other obstacles affluent families can better afford. Encourage sports, music, art, drama, and activities in your program that help teach skills and prepare students for participation in competitive activities in high school. Invite older students to share their positive experiences. Inform parents of the benefits and the need to help their child stick with an activity once it becomes challenging.

Studies show that students who participate in extracurricular activities are less likely to drop out of school. Those most at risk of failure appear to benefit even more from participation. Intervene when parents threaten a child with removal from an activity and explain the long-term benefits compared with the

---

[9] Duckworth, A. (2016). *Grit: The Power of Passion and Perseverance*. New York: Scribner, Simon & Schuster, (p. 226).

probable outcomes of eliminating what may be the most meaningful part of the learning day for a child.

In many cases, extracurricular participation helps students discover and develop a passion for a career. Employers recognize the benefits of being coached and developing the requisite social skills for teamwork. They like a record of commitment.

To demonstrate the benefits of stick-to-it-iveness in extracurriculars, Duckworth developed the Grit Grid. In Figure 4.4, which student is more likely to connect and succeed in college or the workplace, based on their participation in high school activities? Share this visual when working with parents.

Figure 4.4

The Grit Grid

Activity	Grade Level of Participation 9	10	11	12	Achievements, Awards, Leadership Positions
1. *Band*	✓	✓	✓	✓	John Phillip Sousa Award (12) Band President (12)
2. *Student Newspaper*			✓	✓	Editor (12)
3. *Track & Field*	✓	✓	✓	✓	Most improved (10)

List activities (sports, music, drama, volunteering, hobbies, paid work) in which a significant amount of time outside class was devoted.

Activity	Grade Level of Participation 9	10	11	12	Achievements, Awards, Leadership Positions
1. *nothing*					
2.					
3.					

List activities (sports, music, drama, volunteering, hobbies, paid work) in which a significant amount of time outside class was devoted.

from Duckworth, 2016, p. 231

4.5 – Understand How Trauma and Toxic Stress Impacts Behavior

For some kids, as they watch the clock tick past 5:00 p.m., they begin to experience increased levels of anxiety as they imagine what might happen to them when they go home. The chronic stress stemming from the trauma they have experienced at home has likely changed the way their bodies and brains react to the routines and practices of school and afterschool – two of the safest environments they may encounter. For them, negative behavior is a way of surviving and defending themselves. Some freeze (out of fear), others fight, or some even run away (flight).

In the late 90s, data was collected and analyzed from confidential surveys of 17,000 members of Health Maintenance Organizations (HMOs) in Southern California following their physical examinations. The surveys collected information pertaining to participants' childhood experiences, current health status, and behaviors. Known as the original ACEs Study (Adverse Childhood Experiences), this project was a cooperative effort between Kaiser Permanente and the United States Centers for Disease Control and Prevention. It has taken decades for the findings from the study to inform and influence educational practice, but we now know that ACEs is a leading cause of household dysfunction and adult illness. Almost two-thirds of study's participants reported at least one ACE, and more than one in five reported three or more ACEs.[10]

Although Adverse Childhood Experiences (ACEs) can be found throughout all demographic and racial groups, children living in poverty are more likely to have multiple ACEs, compounding the effects of economic insecurity. Add the effects from drugs, violence, homelessness, evictions, and illegal immigration, many school populations enroll children and youth facing extreme levels of trauma.

Afterschool leaders must provide professional development for staff, especially those on the frontline, so that appropriate interventions can enable ACEs children to be receive care and attention in a trauma-sensitive environment. Research shows that trained adults can make a huge difference. The afterschool environment is one of the places where ACEs children find safety and stability.

---

[10] (2016). https://www.cdc.gov/violenceprevention/acestudy/about.html

But if a staff is uninformed, their inadvertent reaction to behaviors may further exacerbate a child's attitude and behavior as well as their mental and physical health.

Planning Tips

1. Review the 10-question ACEs survey. Consult with school officials if there is a suspicion of ACEs to align supports and services.
2. Follow mandated reporting procedures for suspected child abuse or neglect.
3. Revisit zero-tolerant policies. Excessive punishments can retraumatize children and reinforce continuing patterns of bad choices and negativity.
4. Allow trained staff to have flexibility in de-escalating tense situations rather than requiring them to follow strict disciplinary codes.
5. Address children's potential food and clothing scarcities.
6. Cultivate a spirit of empathy, not sympathy.
7. Acknowledge feelings.
8. Provide support to adult caregivers who become role models helping ACEs children develop resilience and compassion.
9. Be authentic when interacting with traumatized kids. They know phoniness.
10. Review Chapter 2 in *Teaching Grit and Mindset in Afterschool Programs: What students, staff, and parents should know and be able to do*. Address the reflective questions and discussion topics at the chapter's end.

The original ACEs survey can be found in Appendix 2.

4.6 – Create an "Adam Plan"

Some kids (often those with an ACEs background) gain a disreputable reputation which they seem unwilling or unable to shake. When a problem develops on the play area or in the restroom, they always seem to be there. They are blamed for incidents when sometimes it was the fault of others. Reinforcing their damaged self-esteems, nothing these children attempt to do appears to put them on the right foot. They lack the social skills and self-discipline to keep their mouths shut and hands to themselves. When an adult looks the other way, they antagonize their peers – or so they stand accused. When adults investigate, "Adam" always appears to have been the one to provoke others.

Tightly structuring the movements of such a child to avoid situations where physical and verbal contact with peers takes place will reduce problems – and provide the challenged child with a respite from detentions or other consequences. As an example, adult supervision in proximity greatly reduces the frequency of "he said, she said" responses from peers. Should a conflict develop, the adult can quickly help mediate and resolve it. Unidentified bullies who may have enjoyed initiating problems and then deflect blame toward "Adam" learn to play somewhere else and the accusations by other students will likely stop. The one-on-one attention from an adult can have immeasurable positive effects on "Adam."

The "Adam Plan" works best when other students are unaware of the reasons why he is always in proximity of an adult.

Staff buy-in and detail-planning are essential to the success of this plan. But the results can be measured by less time resolving nuisance conflicts, improved attitude and reputation, and increase academic gains – for "Adam" and his peers.

Nothing effective happens in an
elementary or middle level afterschool program
without the endorsement and support
of the site-director.

– Paul Young

Dealing with the Non-Stop Talker

Some kids can't help it. They talk too much. Sometimes, their behavior becomes rude and sets off a control struggle between the student and adult. Consider the following scenario.

Skippy is a hyperactive 3rd grader. Most days, he is eager to participate, play a set of bells (glockenspiel) during music time, and respond to the teacher without much concern. However, at times when asked to stop playing, he refuses. When in this mood, he often talks out loud while the teacher tries to give directions. He can become defiant and interact with the teacher in ways that make the other students uncomfortable and the teacher upset.

Which is better?

Scenario 1

1st offense – Teacher gives Skippy the look indicating he is to make better choices and correct his behavior.

2nd offense – Skippy continues to play and talk. Teacher corrects Skippy in front of his classmates. Teacher asks him not to play.

3rd offense – Skippy plays random notes even louder than before. He is testing the teacher's patience. Teacher warns Skippy that if he does not comply, he will be sent to the program site-director.

4th offense – Skippy appears to purposefully disobey. Immediate referral is made to the site-director.

Scenario 2

(a chair is pre-placed next to the teacher before class)

1st offense - Teacher gives Skippy the look indicating he is to make better choices and correct his behavior.

2nd offense – Skippy continues to play and talk. Teacher corrects Skippy in front of his classmates. He is warned that if he does not play correctly, he will be moved to sit in the chair and play.

3rd offense – Skippy plays random notes even louder than before. He is testing the teacher's patience. Teacher moves Skippy to the chair, allows him to continue to play.

4th offense – Skippy talks out loud when the teacher gives directions. Teacher takes mallets and tells Skippy to sit and play silently with "imaginary" mallets.

It's much more fun to play with the other kids than to sit next to the teacher without mallets. Skippy's behavior will likely change if the teacher remains calm, allows him to regain some self-control, and does not provoke a battle.

Program site-directors do not want or need to handle every challenging interaction between students and adults. Students observing the first scenario will soon figure out the that teacher has weak management skills.

Frontline staff should bring good news to the site-director. When program leaders commonly experience staff sharing information about something that's going well, it makes it much easier for them to provide their assistance when staff members really need their help.

4.7 – Encourage Children to Draw

The Washington, DC-based, Arts Education Partnership's 2002 release, *Critical Links*, summarizes the results of sixty-two research studies that examined the effects of arts learning on students' social and academic skills. The research studies covered each of the art forms and has been widely used to help make the case that learning in the arts is academic, basic, and comprehensive.

Use drawing as a creative intervention to counter negative behavior. Some kids can listen, learn, and draw at the same time. Many will learn better when they can doodle or draw a picture. Those with photographic memories will visualize words, graphs, pictures, and illustrations in their texts. Allow them to draw – it supports an important learning style for numerous students.

Drawing reduces the amount of inappropriate behaviors that accompany boredom.

4.8 – Provide Staff with Support

Afterschool = hard work! (see p. 1)

Before a flight can take off, an attendant must inform passengers about the process of placing oxygen masks on themselves before placing one on a young child. At first glance, it seems instinctive to protect a child at all costs. But if you've lost oxygen and passed out, you can't help the child.

Likewise, if adults working in the busy, complex, and often tiring environment of afterschool don't care for themselves, they will burn themselves out and be unable to be effective in their work. Afterschool professionals must be in great physical and mental shape. When you allow yourself to become mentally or physically depleted, kids will gain control.

The most common maladies that negatively impact adult performance are stress and depression. For some, complications from health conditions and medications make them tired. Bad dieting and poor nutritional habits also contribute. Just as with the children, a fruit or vegetable snack might be an important afternoon boost.

Afterschool programs should adopt a wellness plan – for adults as well as students.[11] That plan can support:

- development of daily individual or group exercise activities.
- tobacco cessation support groups.
- nutrition education.
- weight control support.

Runners learn how to pace themselves for races. They also train methodically and take care of their bodies. They know that expending energies too quickly and failing to satisfactorily refresh themselves will negatively impact performance. Afterschool professionals must learn those lessons as well.

4.9 – Solve the Homework Conundrums

- "The dog ate my homework."
- "I know I had it in my bookbag last night."
- "I leave my homework to the last minute, because then I will be older and wiser."

Teachers have heard these and many, many more. Homework has been a source of contention for decades.

Before you decide a program policy regarding homework, first review the Board of Education policies that are applicable to your students. If those policies state that homework is an expectation, you are unwise to be unsupportive. There are procedures for changing board policies you do not like.

Some teachers include homework when they weight grades. Some do not. Regardless, the children in your program who tend to exhibit the most negative behaviors are likely to be those whose teachers never receive homework.

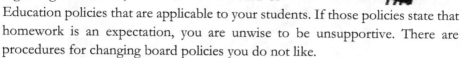

[11] Review NAA's HEPA Standards at https://naaweb.org/resources/naa-hepa-standards

Planning Tips

1. Homework is best when it is designed to support individualized student learning. Consult with students' teachers and plan ways to support their expectations and agree on strategies to share responsibility for success.
2. Utilize the 20-minute meeting with the principal to monitor homework progress, completion, and satisfaction (see 3.14).
3. Develop foolproof plans for collecting homework assignments from teachers before the transition to afterschool and for collecting it once completed. If needed, adults can take assignments to teachers at school the next day until a time in which the student(s) can display adequate self-responsibility.
4. Request permission for afterschool staff to observe teachers to become familiar with their instructional methods and preferred procedures for homework completion.
5. Communicate expectations and share practices and responsibilities of the afterschool program with parents.
6. Document your efforts and celebrate success.

4.10 – Create a "Purple Cow" Effect for Your Program

If you were driving down a highway and saw a purple cow standing in a field within a group of black, brown, or white cows, you'd probably stop your car, take a picture, and share your surprise, excitement, and sense of wonder with all your friends. You'd share the picture on social media and talk about the experience for days.

There are countless numbers of black, brown, and white cows. What about purple cows?[12] If you saw one, it would be remarkable! Different! Attention-making! Other people would be curious and want to see it, too!

The problem with afterschool programs (and schools) is that they are viewed like cows – much the same, bland colors, and often sometimes less than remarkable. What if you set out to purposefully change that perception? Does the act of striving to attain remarkable customer satisfaction model positive or negative behavior?

Planning Tips

1. If someone calls the afterschool program, does the person responding create a remarkable conversational exchange? If not, how might that be improved? How many phone rings are heard before someone picks up?
2. If someone visits your program, are they greeted and communicated with in ways that help them leave feeling good? You'll know if they share that remarkable experience with others.
3. If a parent visits the program, what do they see, hear, feel, and smell? Are they greeted with a smile? Do they feel like they are given your full attention? What makes them perceive that your program is different and sets it apart from others?
4. Spend time during a staff in-service meeting discussing this concept. Brainstorm ideas (see Figure 4.10, p. 105). Whatever "purple" ideas are agreed upon and implemented must first have staff buy-in and become genuine goals. People see through gimmicks very quickly.

[12] Read Godin, S. (2003). *Purple Cow: Transform Your Business by Being Remarkable*. New York: Portfolio/Penguin Group.

McDonald's and other businesses that are frequented by the public face similar challenges of creating remarkable experiences. People are conditioned to expect a level of quality, but you know a visit is truly remarkable when you see it, and you know when it is not. The site-director sets the tone. How you dress, your sense of style, the presence you command, the way you motivate others, and the way you make people feel all contribute to the remarkable effect.

What is the brand of your program? It is a combination of ambitious aspirations that makes it remarkable.

Kindness is contagious - awesomeness is a choice!

Q. - What is a key indicator of a remarkable afterschool program?
A. - When during dismissal, a child tells their parent they can't wait to come back to your afterschool program tomorrow.

Color me purple!

See related resources in Appendices 3 and 4

Figure 4.10

Everyone can contribute to your "Purple Cow" initiatives. Creatively recreate a handout (as seen on this page) to meet your needs that is available for everyone. Give a high-five and a shout-out for good service actions and behavior. Positivity breeds success.

Give an amazing student a
HIGH-FIVE
for their marvelous,
wonderful work at
Main Street Afterschool Program.
Fill out the form below. Your
message will be given to the
student tomorrow. Please give the
completed form to the receptionist
before you leave today.

From:

Summary

Aesop's fable about the tortoise and the hare seems applicable to conclude this chapter. Students and staff in afterschool programs who move at lightning pace through the activities of the day often become tired like the hare. Instead, a steady pace like the tortoise saves energy for the ending part of any race or activity. Students respond well to effective, steady pacing. They'll take advantage of adults who move too fast or too slow. If there are cracks in the wall, they will find them.

Basketball players know that games are won in the second half, not the first. Only those teams with the endurance and energy to persevere throughout the game and season will consistently achieve success.

Working in and leading an afterschool program is similar to those sports examples. Endurance is an important personal and professional quality, and it is essential that afterschool professionals learn to maintain steady and consistent levels of effort throughout each day – and all year long.

Checklist IV - Second Half (After 5:00 p.m.)
Structural Analysis and Assessment

Goal 1	Indicators	A	B	C	D	NA
There is evidence of student learning.	a) Students have a choice in their learning activities with staff support.					
	b) Planning and instruction to meet students' multiple learning styles and needs is evident.					
	c) There are positive results from the implementation of a code of conduct.					
	d) Technology is evident that supports efficacy.					
	e) Students eat a balanced, nutritious supper.					

Goal 2	Indicators	A	B	C	D	NA
Instructional time in this block remains as effective as that right after school.	a) Staff members are observed to have energy and enthusiasm.					
	b) Healthy snacks are available.					
	c) There is evidence of planning and input from all staff.					
	d) Staff behavioral norms are observed.					
	e) Behavioral referrals are handled effectively.					
	f) The number of improper behavior/attitude referrals maintains consistency with other parts of the day.					

Goal 3	Indicators	A	B	C	D	NA
There is effective planning for homework completion and parent communication.	a) Varied communication needs are addressed.					
	b) Emergency planning is evident.					
	c) A variety of activities for students is planned.					
	d) Minimal time is wasted moving students from one point to another.					
	e) Movement through hallways is quiet and orderly.					
	f) Organization is evident.					

Checklist IV - Second Half (After 5:00 p.m.) Structural Analysis and Assessment						
Goal 3	**Indicators**	**A**	**B**	**C**	**D**	**NA**
	g) Little time is wasted between recreational, restroom breaks, meals, and instructional activities.					
Goal 4	**Indicators**	**A**	**B**	**C**	**D**	**NA**
All staff members interact and communicate with students and parents in a positive manner.	a) A code of conduct is reinforced					
	b) Student dismissals are managed according to regulations.					
	c) A sense of order, consistency, and cooperation among staff is observable.					

Summary Notes:

Identified Norms of Afterschool Program Structure:

Checklist IV - Second Half (After 5:00 p.m.)
Structural Analysis and Assessment

Areas of Strength:

List… (ex. IV-1b, etc.)

Targeted Areas for Improvement:

List… (ex. IV-2b, etc.)

Adult Behavioral Norms Needed to Achieve Expectations:

Recommendations:

V

Endings (Dismissal Time and Wrap-Up of the Year)

Ideas, Advice, and Reflections that Reinforce Positive Behaviors When Things Wind Down

Our greatest weakness lies in giving up. The most certain way to succeed is always to try just one more time.

- Thomas A. Edison

Introduction

The school day (or year) may come to an end, but not the responsibilities of the staff. Experience shows that dismissal can be one of the most dangerous and high-risk times of the day, for students as well as adults. It is essential that the afterschool staff identify the small structural issues that support and facilitate a safe and efficient dismissal of students – before leaving themselves.

To ascertain the validity of that statement, visit afterschool programs (or any school) and watch what happens. Where students exit the facility in an orderly manner, adults will be visible. They will be observed greeting parents, talking with bus drivers, planning with afterschool personnel, and releasing all students safely to the care of a parent or guardian.

Elsewhere, adults may appear to be racing the students out of the building in a rush to the parking lot. Who is left to care for the child whose parent is late arriving? Who answers questions about homework? Who hears complaints or discusses issues with concerned parents? Which program appears to place the interest of students first? Where would you rather your *own* child attend?

The end of the day and year is an important time to reflect, assess the success of the program's practices and procedures, and plan for the next day or year. This takes time. Don't rush. Assure that all the loose ends are tied. Reflection is an integral part of the planning process. Clean up the messes before starting afresh. Then celebrate the end.

Leave no children behind.
The staff can relax only after each child is safely released to the care of a parent or designee.

Visit Other Programs

As expressed in 3.13, inviting guests to your program is a positive practice. Similarly, a visitation to another afterschool program is an effective professional learning activity which unfortunately is often overlooked. Through your contacts in your state or national professional associations, make a friend and connect with them at their site. Visit while the program is in session. You'll be surprised at the number of ideas you will pick up that will improve your work. Include as many staff members as possible. And don't neglect to visit and support your colleagues at sites in your local program organization. Visit, collaborate, share, learn, and grow together!

5.1 – Establish a Positive Pick-up Environment and Process

One of the best times to establish positive relationships and affirm good behavior with students and their parents is during dismissal. But, throw in some inclement weather, and everyone's level of patience and frustration is tested. If parents enter an environment that is cold, chaotic, and unwelcoming, they take their kids and walk away feeling little connection to the program. However, if they get the "purple cow" treatment, they will leave and spread word of the remarkable experience, specifically talking about the positive behaviors that emanate from your program.

Planning Tips

1. Designate a greeter. Welcome parents using first and last names – and smile!
2. Share a positive about each child with their parent. Sometimes, saying something so the child can also hear it sets a positive tone that can change a child's attitude forever.
3. Develop a smooth flow in and out of your program area. Is there adequate parking and security? If you have buses, is there enough space for safe, supervised loading and unloading with plans that avoid congestion with parents driving cars?
4. Specify expectations for students who may have permission to walk home. Communicate the time and place when the program's obligatory supervision comes to an end and parental responsibilities begin.
5. Assign adequate staff to supervise the dismissal process.
6. Clearly delineate in your student/parent handbook the processes and expectations that facilitate a smooth, safe dismissal and pick-up of all children.
7. Develop a plan for supervision of children whose parents are late and arrive after closing time. It will happen, emergencies occur. How you decide to handle these situations will test you and reflect your commitment to promoting positive behaviors, especially with those who are chronically late.

5.2 – Ride School Buses

If your program provides busing, program administrators and staff can establish positive relations with drivers by occasionally riding the bus. Whether your program is in a rural, suburban, or urban setting, much can be gleaned from a bus ride with students. Not only will you be able to observe their behavior in that setting, but you'll learn where they live and gain a perception of the home and neighborhood environment from which they come. Bus drivers will appreciate the acknowledgement of the challenges they face. They'll welcome your assistance and support with management of student behavior. And they'll provide you with their unique understandings of children, their families, and your community if you listen.

Do you desire better relations with transportation personnel? Invite drivers for coffee and conversation. Want to reduce bus conduct referrals? Just ride, observe what happens, listen, and show your support. Proactively becoming involved with transportation will reduce the negativity associated with bus conduct referrals.

The only thing harder than managing a bunch of students is to do it while driving a bus.

– Todd Whitaker
author, Univ. of Missouri professor

5.3 – Walk Students Home

From time to time, surprise parents and citizens within the neighborhood by walking students to their home. It won't take long, and the public relations established through shared learning opportunities will be memorable.

Expect various reactions and receptions. Some parents will graciously welcome you, others will not. Regardless, what you might observe and learn about a student's home life will likely influence your expectations. You will no longer chastise a fourth-grade student for failure to complete homework at the kitchen table after you see the child's home has no kitchen! From the simple act of walking students to their home, many afterschool professionals gain insights that influence their planning and structure of their program – and perhaps the way they look at kids forever. They develop affirmative interventions during time before or after school for expectations that cannot be provided at home.

5.4 – Establish Curb Appeal

Imagine you are a visitor to your program. You park your car and walk up the sidewalk. What would you see? Weeds? Flowers? Broken sidewalks? Doors needing paint or cleaning? Manicured lawns? Cigarette butts everywhere? Multiple indicators of welcome – or the impersonal "Visitors Must Report to the Office" sign? When students, staff, and parents display pride in your program, it will always be clean and well maintained. Curb appeal creates an impression about our program. It reflects a positive culture.

Cleaning is an ongoing necessity. Even if you are housed in a school with custodial services provided, if you have program pride, you assume some tidiness duties yourself.

A good practice is to establish a daily, weekly, monthly, and annual review of cleaning and maintenance needs. Get rid of the clutter. Be creative in developing an attractive, welcoming, yet functional entrance to your program.

Students will develop a sense of pride in the program if they are invited to help with developing curb appeal and keeping their area clean. Plant flowers and gardens. Create colorful displays. Parents will love to see pictures or positive videos being displayed of students (especially their own) while they wait at the dismissal area. Encourage students to make those videos.

5.5 – Eliminate Gum

At the request of custodians, many program leaders forbid gum chewing. If you question why, join them as they work to remove dried gum from carpet or underneath chairs. That should help justify the ban for anyone in doubt.

Moreover, chewing gum while working seems contrary to the rules of etiquette and professionalism. Set a positive example for children.

5.6 – Alert Bosses About Potential Problems

Before going home for the day (or year), take time to reflect about all that has transpired. If you sense any anxiety about an interaction or encounter with a student, parent, teacher, or volunteer that might result in a call to the principal, tell her about it, send an explanatory email, or leave a note before you go home. Principals should follow the same practice alerting the afterschool program and site-director of potentially tough issues *before* a parent or community member contacts them.

This is simply a courteous practice that can solidify your support, assuming your actions were appropriate, and help your superiors better understand both sides to an issue and defend your actions. It is not good practice for the boss to hear complaints and learn of problems from others. Everyone makes mistakes, and even the most veteran staff member can occasionally be blindsided by a developing issue. Just make it a practice to reflect, be aware of others' perceptions, and keep all your bases covered. It's those that appear to be clueless who are most difficult to support and place the administrator in the most tenuous of positions.

5.7 – Be a Master Motivator

The easiest way to become a master motivator is to surround yourself with motivated people. But that is not always possible. However, everyone can develop skills and characteristics that inspire others. Motivation spreads like a virus. Start with staff in-service and gain buy-in for their commitment to focus efforts and share best practices. Before leaving for the day, staff should adopt the practice of sharing a motivational moment rather than something that went wrong. Part of your end-of-year reflections should be devoted to assessment of motivation – students, staff, parents.

Don't complain that students or adults lack motivation. If that's what you think, take a long look in the mirror. Maybe they simply don't want to follow you. Those who reflect are continuously working to find ways to be even better. It is most desirable when the entire staff works and learns as a team.

Planning Tips

When your staff discusses motivation and works to increase it among students (and each other) within your program, consider these suggestions:

1. Be generous with your praise of others.
2. Make sure your integrity is above reproach.
3. Expect the best and work continuously to achieve positive results.
4. Maintain your content knowledge and instructional skills so they are second to none.
5. Continuously establish clear and achievable goals.
6. Look for others' strengths and good qualities instead of focusing on their weaknesses.
7. Delegate responsibilities and grow each person's capacities and professionalism.
8. Develop new leaders.
9. Keep an open mind and be willing to change.
10. Have a vision of what you hope to achieve and make sure that others can visualize themselves in that same future. Get out front and pull others with you rather than pushing them from behind. Make sure you have purpose and direction in everything you do.
11. Listen to people and actually hear what they say.
12. Provide caring, sincere, and confident feedback. Mean what you say! Don't be two-faced.
13. Cooperate and collaborate with others.
14. Ask questions and clarify what you don't understand.
15. Limit criticism and focus on developing positive problem-solving skills.
16. Show people you have a genuine, warm personality and that you care.
17. Demonstrate continuous energy and vitality.
18. Show enthusiasm for learning and mastering new skills.
19. Become an articulate speaker and writer.
20. Practice what you preach.
21. Set a personal example that will attract others who want to work hard, achieve excellence, exceed your goals, and surpass their own possibilities.

5.8 – Toot Your Own Horn

Advertising and promotional events are important for afterschool programs and the individuals who work in them. In order to sustain afterschool programs, the professionals working in them must convincingly tell their stories. The challenge is tooting your own horn without becoming overbearing.

The site-director needs to make sure their subordinates receive recognition for their work. Use every opportunity and means available to give a shout-out for positive endeavors. If you create a team effort, you'll realize success stems not from an "I" but rather a "We" effort.

Tooting your own program's horn is not arrogant or selfish if it celebrates how you've helped kids, their families, and your community. However, be careful not to assume all credit for a child's success. Children spend a good part of their learning time with other teachers. Share credit. Adopt the mantra "sharing the responsibility for success."

Without promotion, something terrible happens—nothing.

- P.T. Barnum

5.9 – Align the School and Afterschool Program Learning Opportunities

For nearly 20 years, nearly two-thirds of American principals have reported some type of afterschool program associated with their school (NAESP, 2005). To attain and sustain quality, the support and endorsement of a principal who understands and supports a program mission and shares responsibility for casting the vision is essential. It is also important for developing positive behaviors (NAESP, 2005). Most principals will welcome programs into their schools and work collaboratively with the afterschool team to extend and enrich learning time for all children, especially those needing extra time to close learning gaps.

However, program effectiveness is often hindered by attitudes, space, and turf issues. Students fail to benefit from expanded learning opportunities when communication doesn't exist or breaks down between the school staff and afterschool personnel. In my work with afterschool professionals, the perceived lack of attention from principals – respect and recognition for how afterschool supports the school day – was cited as the primary reason site-directors became negative. That attitude was then reflected by staff, and eventually picked up by students.

To help support the communication between principals and afterschool professionals and focus on the critical conversations they must have to promote positive relationships, the National Association of Elementary School Principals (NAESP) released *Leading After-School Communities: What Principals Should Know and Be Able to Do in 2005.* To compliment that resource, I published *Principal Matters: 101 Tips for Creating Collaborative Relationships Between After-School Programs and School Leaders* in 2009. Both books have been used successfully to build strong connections and guide the collaborative work between school and afterschool. A planning resource from the NAESP publication can be found in Appendix 5.

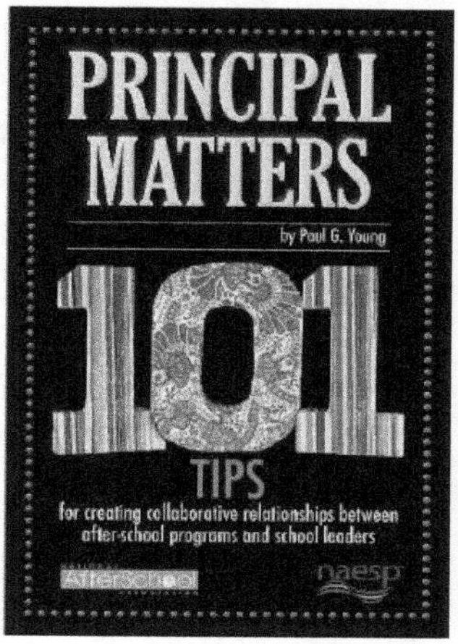

Principals have the power and influence to make sure the connection between school and afterschool is positively developed and sustained. They can assure that seamless learning experiences are developed for their students. Their periodic visits to the afterschool program can motivate the students and afterschool staff. Their visits, as well as others from the students' teachers, are wonderful opportunities to discuss and continuously refine alignment strategies.

Summary

A typical school year is a whirlwind of activities. Staff members' time is consumed planning, teaching, intervening, responding to students' and parents' questions, attending meetings and conferences, conducting observations, making phone calls, and interacting with people. Time flies. No wonder people are tired at the end of a day and need a summer break.

It is important to recognize the value of having a life and interests away from work. Structure your day and allow time for *you*. Avoid burnout. Exercise, visit friends, volunteer at a nursing home, read, or shop. Do something that helps draw you away from the stressors that have accumulated throughout the day. Enjoy a hobby. Take care of yourself. Get enough rest for the next day.

Don't forget to maintain a good sense of humor. What might have seemed so critical or important today will likely be funnier tomorrow and months from now. Shake off the problems and stress. Laugh, smile, and enjoy your family and time at home.

I was fortunate to have worked nearly 20 years as an elementary principal. During much of that time, I also served my peers in elected leadership positions with the Ohio Association of Elementary School Administrators (OAESA) and the National Association of Elementary School Principals (NAESP). Developing strong links between schools and afterschool programs was an important focus of my work. Upon retirement, that work continued as a board member and as President of the National AfterSchool Association (NAA). By leading collaborative trainings across the country with NAESP and NAA, I learned that principals have great respect for afterschool programming, especially where leaders and their staffs can develop opportunities that expand student learning in a way that does not simply extend and replicate what happens during the school day. I learned that principals admired competent program leaders who could manage students with autonomy and yet would keep them informed should problems develop. They appreciated and respected the connections that afterschool personnel developed with parents that they were not able to construct. Mostly, they were proud to share responsibility for success in environments in which the mission and vision were mutually developed and positive structures and behaviors were taught, retaught, and established as norms.

My experience shows me that the tips and advice shared within this book – and others that you and your staff will learn in your unique setting – *do* work. Developing a positive culture is a process. Realizing your vision takes time, grit, and a growth mindset. Success is achieved from a team effort. I witnessed hundreds of exemplary examples throughout the nation, in my state, and in my home programs.

Use the checklists at the end of each chapter to guide your staff's reflective activities and discussion. Use them in a way that works for you, your staff, and your setting. I wish you success. Pay it forward, and let others know what you learn!

Checklist V - Endings (Dismissal Time and Wrap-Up of the Year)—Structural Analysis and Assessment

Goal 1	Indicators	A	B	C	D	NA
There is evidence of planning for a safe and orderly dismissal.	a) All staff members assume responsibility for supervision of assigned students in designated areas.					
	b) Students are dismissed to a parent or guardian and transfer is documented.					
	c) Accommodations for bus riders are a priority.					
	d) Staff members ride buses.					
	e) Drop-off locations at bus stops are safe and supervised.					
	f) Students who walk home are safe and supervised.					
	g) Safety considerations for everyone during dismissal times are observable.					
	h) Staff members are aware of where students live.					
	i) Clutter is nonexistent.					
	j) Materials are inventoried, stored, and records accurately completed.					

Goal 2	Indicators	A	B	C	D	NA
Discipline and behavioral expectations are well-planned and taught.	a) Parent communication has taken place and support gained.					
	b) Consequences are planned to positively change student behaviors.					
	c) Problems are reported to appropriate officials (principal/teachers) before the end of the day.					

Goal 3	Indicators	A	B	C	D	NA
Staff interaction with parents, bus drivers, and after-school personnel is positive.	a) School-to-home communication with parents is positive.					
	b) Preventative problem-solving is observed.					
	c) Attention is given to customer service.					
	d) Staff members walk students home and make positive phone calls.					

Checklist V - Endings (Dismissal Time and Wrap-Up of the Year)—Structural Analysis and Assessment						
Goal 4	**Indicators**	**A**	**B**	**C**	**D**	**NA**
Staff interacts and communicates with students and parents in a positive manner.	a) A code of conduct is reinforced.					
	b) A sense of order, consistency, and cooperation among staff is observable.					
	c) There is a plan for determining schedules, attendance, and student registration that is supported by parents and teachers.					

Summary Notes:

Identified Norms of Afterschool Program Structure:

Checklist V - Endings (Dismissal Time and Wrap-Up of the Year)—Structural Analysis and Assessment Areas of Strength:

Areas of Strength:

List… (ex. V-2b, etc.)

Targeted Areas for Improvement:

List… (ex. V-2b, etc.)

Adult Behavioral Norms Needed to Achieve Expectations:

Recommendations:

Rubric Explanation of the Structural Analysis and Assessment Levels

Master Level: (A) Proactively, the entire afterschool program staff continuously discusses and is aware of specific details of structural issues, analyzes strengths and weaknesses in various settings, teaches structural concepts to students in various settings, understands the interconnected relationships between issues, and agrees upon norms of adult and student behaviors. Such behaviors are observable each day. Qualitative measures of program climate and productivity are exceptionally high and sustained over time. **Structure is observable continuously each day.**

Professional Level: (B) In response to problems, most of the afterschool program staff discusses and is aware of specific details of most issues, analyzes strengths and weaknesses in most settings, teaches structural concepts to students in most settings, understands the interconnected relationships between most issues, and agrees upon most norms of adult and student behavior. Such behaviors are observable most of the time. Qualitative measures of program climate and productivity are high and sustained most of the time. **Structure is observable most of the time each day.**

Inconsistent Level: (C) In response to problems, some of the afterschool program staff discusses and is aware of specific details of some issues, but not all. The staff sometimes analyzes strengths and weaknesses and periodically teaches structural concepts to students in most settings. Different levels of agreement of norms of adult and student behavior exist. Desired student and adult behaviors are observable some of the time. Qualitative measures of school climate and productivity vary. The entire school staff would benefit from professional development. **Structure is observable each day from some, not others.**

Ineffective Level: (D) It is seldom that the entire afterschool program staff discusses or is aware of any type of structural issues, analyzes strengths and weaknesses, or teaches structural concepts to students in various settings. Inappropriate student and adult behaviors are observable each day. Time is wasted. Qualitative measures of program climate and productivity indicate low student and staff morale, dissatisfaction, and underachievement. The entire afterschool staff needs assistance. Professional staff development from an outside, independent source is recommended. **Inappropriate observations are made each day.**

Not Observable: (NA) Evidence that the entire afterschool program staff discusses any specific details of structural issues, analyzes strengths or weaknesses, teaches structural concepts to students, understands the interconnected relationships between issues, or agrees upon norms of adult and student behaviors are not observable. An issue may not be observable or applicable because of the uniqueness of a setting or other circumstance. **Observations of structure are not made or are not applicable.**

The Five Stages of Afterschool Instructional Mastery

1. **Pretend** – Ever watch young children when they come home from school? One of the first things many want to do is *play school.* They are pretending to teach like an adult they admire. They enter a fantasy world. They become hooked on school. Young afterschool professionals resemble that attitude at first – their work may appear to be pretend-like. They imagine they know what they are doing. Reality, however, lets them know that working with young children is hard work, and they must better prepare to attain success and satisfaction.
2. **Prepare** – This stage involves formal study of theory and practice, observation, and countless hours of professional learning. Without devoting time and commitment at this level, the output is still pretend-like.
3. **Practice** – Once you can imagine yourself working with young people, and you have adequately studied, you must put into practice what you've learned. Like learning to drive a car, there are fantasy games that can be played, seat-work that must be completed, followed with hours of run-throughs, repetition, trial and error, reflection, and reworking some of the finer points of delivering instruction.

At any stage, individuals may find it necessary and helpful to go back and strengthen their skills at a lower level. Without a solid base of continuous support, the highest levels are unattainable.

4. **Perform** – After hours of practicing their craft, which can add up to being years, instructors reach a level where they feel they can execute skills with confidence. They command a stage and function in ways that lead to high levels of accomplishment.
5. **Perfect** – Those who commit the time and work the hardest gain respect and recognition and function at levels that appear to others to be perfection. They deliver instruction with ease, confidently in a flawless manner, as if on auto-pilot. They are afterschool professionals.

Appendix 1

The Afterschool Program Culture Survey

Directions: Please indicate the degree to which each statement describes conditions in your afterschool program.

1=Strongly Disagree 2=Disagree 3=Undecided 4=Agree 5= Strongly Agree

The Questions		1	2	3	4	5
1.	The program mission is known and supported.					
2.	A program vision is clear and agreed upon by staff.					
3.	Planning aligns with program and school goals/targets.					
4.	Program leaders value staff's ideas and judgment.					
5.	Staff attends seminars, trainings, and conferences.					
6.	Professional development is valued by the staff.					
7.	Visitations to other programs occur regularly.					
8.	Trust is evident throughout the program.					
9.	Staff regularly seeks ideas from each other.					
10.	Staff problem-solving skills are evident.					
11.	All staff share in decision-making processes.					
12.	Common expectations exist for student behavior.					
13.	Staff communication is effective.					
14.	Leaders offer praise for effective work.					
15.	Collaboration and cooperative learning are evident.					
16.	Self-improvement is a prominent goal of staff.					
17.	Staff and students display autonomy.					
18.	Students demonstrate learning/behavior targets.					
19.	Students demonstrate respect for staff and peers.					
20.	Parents trust professional judgments of staff.					
21.	Leaders and staff value program improvement.					
22.	Disagreements and conflict are handled professionally.					
23.	Parent involvement, support, and respect is evident.					
24.	Program positivity and successes are celebrated.					
25.	The program is known and valued in the community.					

Appendix 2

Finding Your ACE Score Answer yes or no to the ten questions listed.		
While you were growing up, during your first 18 years of life:	Yes	No
1. Did a parent or other adult in the household often or very often swear at you, insult you, put you down, or humiliate you or act in a way that made you afraid that you might be physically hurt?		
2. Did a parent or other adult in the household often or very often push, grab, slap, or throw something at you or ever hit you so hard that you had marks or were injured?		
3. Did an adult person at least 5 years older than you ever touch or fondle you or have you touch their body in a sexual way or attempt or actually have oral, anal, or vaginal intercourse with you?		
4. Did you often or very often feel that no one in your family loved you or thought you were important or special or your family didn't look out for each other, feel close to each other, or support each other?		
5. Did you often or very often feel that you didn't have enough to eat, had to wear dirty clothes, and had no one to protect you or your parents were too drunk or high to take care of you or take you to the doctor if you needed it?		
6. Were your parents ever separated or divorced?		
7. Was your mother or stepmother often or very often pushed, grabbed, slapped, or had something thrown at her or sometimes, often, or very often kicked, bitten, hit with a fist, or hit with something hard or ever repeatedly hit at least a few minutes or threatened with a gun or knife?		
8. Did you live with anyone who was a problem drinker or alcoholic or who used street drugs?		
9. Was a household member depressed or mentally ill, or did a household member attempt suicide?		
10. Did a household member go to prison?		
Add up the number of "Yes" answers. That is your ACE score.		

Source: http://acestudy.org/index.html

Appendix 3

50 Positive Comments to Make with Children and Youth

1.	You made a good decision.	26.	It's okay to feel bad.
2.	Thank you for doing that.	27.	You show great curiosity.
3.	That action makes me smile.	28.	I like how you share.
4.	I understand why you feel that way.	29.	That's a very mature way to act.
5.	That is a great idea.	30.	I like your enthusiasm.
6.	You are right, I am wrong.	31.	That shows good judgment.
7.	I appreciate your effort.	32.	You choose your words well.
8.	I admire how you did that.	33.	That is good logic.
9.	Let's try it your way.	34.	I like how you never give up.
10.	I believe in you.	35.	You are a good team player.
11.	I like how you are listening.	36.	Keep up the good work.
12.	Thank you for being a friend to ______________.	37.	Thank you for following the Code of Conduct.
13.	I appreciate your willingness to try something new.	38.	That's a great display of cooperation.
14.	You are being very brave.	39.	You are always so upbeat.
15.	It's okay to make a mistake.	40.	Thank you for listening.
16.	Thank you for waiting patiently.	41.	Thank you for getting your work done on time.
17.	I like that attitude.	42.	You look very nice today.
18.	You have a lovely smile.	43.	You are a valued classmate.
19.	Congratulations!	44.	You are well-prepared.
20.	That's very responsible.	45.	You can do it - I know!
21.	You are very courteous.	46.	Thanks for double checking.
22.	That is a great goal.	47.	That's very helpful.
23.	Very well said.	48.	That's very considerate.
24.	Good use of your free time.	49.	You should be proud of that.
25.	Thank you for following my directions.	50.	You have a good sense of humor.

Appendix 4

In this afterschool program, it is "cool" to...

- ☐ **wear a smile.**
- ☐ **say please and thank you.**
- ☐ **be kind to others.**
- ☐ **observe the safety rules.**
- ☐ **show respect and get respect.**
- ☐ **know and use everyone's name.**
- ☐ **speak in complete sentences.**
- ☐ **share.**
- ☐ **be a team player.**
- ☐ **learn new skills.**
- ☐ **get things done on time.**
- ☐ **be responsible for actions.**
- ☐ **cooperate.**
- ☐ **work hard.**
- ☐ **try.**

Appendix 5

Responsibility Checklist for the Principal and Afterschool Program Director

Directions: The principal and afterschool program site-director (and coordinators) should complete this checklist together. Review the tasks in Column 1, then indicate who will be responsible – the principal or program director – or whether it will be a shared responsibility. If a responsibility will be shared, decide how it will be shared. It might be advisable to review this checklist 2 or 3 times each year.

Task	Responsibility of the Principal	Responsibility of Afterschool Program Director	Shared Responsibility (indicate how)
1. Secure space for after-school activities.	*Who* *What* *When* *How* *Where*	*Who* *What* *When* *How* *Where*	*Who* *What* *When* *How* *Where*
2. Inform classroom teachers that their classrooms will be used. (don't forget classified staff, particularly custodians)			
3. Provide supplies and materials for after-school programs. (ex. paper, copier, books, computers, postage, laminator)			
4. Handle behavior issues that arise in the after-school program.			
5. Communicate with parents about content of the afterschool program. (develop brochures etc.)			
6. Recruit students for afterschool programs.			
7. Decide which activities will be provided.			

Appendix 5, continued

Responsibility Checklist for the Principal and Afterschool Program Director

Task	Responsibility of the Principal	Responsibility of Afterschool Program Director	Shared Responsibility (indicate how)
8. Involve school staff in curriculum and activity development.			
9. Hire and supervise program staff.			
10. Register/orient program participants.			
11. Communicate with classroom teachers (and parents) about homework.			
12. Provide professional development for afterschool staff.			
13. Manage the afterschool budget.			
14. Collect fees from students and develop/raise program funds.			
15. Develop an evaluation framework; collect and analyze data; share results.			
16. Share information about the program with the school community, Bd. of Ed., and public.			

Adapted from Leading After-School Communities: What Principals Should Know and Be Able to Do, National Association of Elementary School Principals (NAESP), 2006, pp. 44-45, and Beyond the Bell: A Principal's Guide to Effective Afterschool Programs, Learning Point Associates, 2005, pp.26-27.

Appendix 6

Common Non-Verbal Communication Techniques

All afterschool professionals will benefit from a repertoire of silent, recognizable, easy-to-implement gestures or techniques that quickly and effectively communicate messages to students in positive ways.

	The Message	Description
1	**Call to Attention**	There are numerous variations that work, but an easy one is the three-finger countdown. Place a hand in the air and indicate the countdown 3 – 2 – 1 – Quiet.
2.	**Hush!**	The index finger over the lips indicates a signal to stop talking or remain silent.
3.	**Listen!**	Place the fingers of one hand behind an ear, the palm of the hand facing forward. The index finger of the other hand gives the silent signal.
4.	**Focus the Eyes!**	Look at the inattentive student and slowly direct two of your fingers to your eyes messaging that they need to return to task.
5.	**Heads Up!**	Place the fingertips of both hands to the sides of your head to indicate that attention needed.
6.	**Slow Down!**	Use both hands, open palms facing students, and look as if you are quietly pushing away.
7.	**Hurry Up!**	Quickly rotate your index finger in the air to indicate the expression to move along more quickly.
8.	**Wait!**	Placing an index finger to the palm of the other hand indicates wait your turn. Eye contact should be used effectively to accompany this gesture.
9.	**The Silent Vote**	Simple: Thumb up or thumb down
10.	**Way to Go!**	The simple act of silent applause.
11.	**Restroom Signal**	Students can be taught the silent signal of two crossed fingers indicating the need to go to the restroom.
12.	**Thank you!**	A gesture from American Sign Language. Slowly remove your fingertips from your lips, as if blowing a kiss. Can also indicate recognition for good work.

Every effective educator needs to be able to walk into a room and deliver "The Look!" to achieve a myriad of desired results.

Appendix 7

Educational Acronyms

Educators appear to have a language all their own when they are using acronyms. Often, novice afterschool professionals can be caught off-guard if they are uninformed as to what each represents. This is not a comprehensive list, but a good start. If you don't understand the definition, research further. Keep this list handy for staff quizzes and when interviewing new personnel.

	Acronym	**What It Defines**
1.	ADA	Americans with Disabilities Act
2.	ADHD	Attention-Deficit Hyperactive Disorder
3.	CACFP	Child and Adult Care Food Program
4.	CPS	Child Protective Services
5.	DARE	Drug Abuse Resistance Education
6.	ELO	Extended Learning Opportunities (Afterschool)
7.	ESC	Educational Service Center
8.	ESL	English as a Second Language
9.	FAPE	Free Appropriate Public Education
10.	FERPA	Family Education Rights and Privacy Act
11.	IDEA	Individuals with Disabilities Education Improvement Act
12.	IEP	Individualized Educational Program
13.	JFS	Job and Family Services
14.	LD	Learning Disabled, or SLD (Specific Learning Disabilities)
15.	LRE	Least Restrictive Environment
16.	MRDD	Mental Retardation Developmental Disabilities
17.	PBIS	Positive Behavior Interventions and Support
18.	SACC	School-Age Child Care
19.	SFSP	Summer Food Service Program
20.	21stCCLC	21st Century Community Learning Centers (Afterschool)
21.	Title 1	A federally funded program that provides financial assistance through state or local education agencies for schools with high percentages of poor children

Index

2 x 10 Relationship Builder 19

A

administrative support 49
Adverse Childhood Experiences 96
ACEs Study 96
Aesop's fable 106
afterschool programs ... 3, 6, 18, 30, 33, 45, 48, 50, 61, 66, 94, 103, 106, 112, 118, 120, 133
ambitious aspirations 104
Arts Education Partnership 100
assemblies 45
attitude of positivity 82
aural skills 71
avoidance syndrome 82

B

behavioral norms ... 39, 55, 85, 109, 125
belief statement ...*See* mission statement
board of education policies 101
bodily-kinesthetic intelligence 91
boredom 101
break time 4, 57, 83, 84, 85
bullying 66
burnout 100, 120
bus conduct referrals 114

C

cameras 59, 70
clutter 115
code of conduct 15, 16, 17, 23, 131
commonsense 77, 93
community officials 49
conflict management 79
confrontations 68
crisis supervision 70
culture 4, 9, 129
curb appeal 115
customer satisfaction 103

D

discipline 14, 15, 107
dismissal 111, 113, 115, 123
dress codes 33
Duckworth, Angela 94, 95, 143
due-process hearing 16

E

email communication 35
endurance 106
Energy Bus 13, 143
environment 3, 22, 53, 113, 144
extracurricular activities 94

F

frontline staff 99
frustration 20, 92, 113

G

Gardner, Howard 90, 143
Good News Call of the Day 90
gratitude 93
grit 92, 94, 95, 140, 141, 143, 144
growth mindset 95

H

high-five 105
homelessness 2, 96
homework 21, 37, 41, 92, 101, 107, 112, 114, 134, 141
hurtful behavior 66
hygiene 60

I

illegal immigration ... 96
illicit behavior ... 48
inclement weather ... 113
inconsistent level ... 126
initiative ... 93
inside voices ... 60, 83
instructional time ... 41, 42
integrity ... 93
interpersonal intelligence ... 91
intervention ... 2, 39, 43, 58, 65, 100
intimidation ... 2, 66
intrapersonal intelligence ... 91

L

lines ... 28
linguistic intelligence ... 91
logical-mathematical intelligence ... 91

M

manners ... 60, 77
Marzano, Robert ... 17, 144
master level performance ... 126
meals & snacks ... 4, 57, 83, 84, 85
mealtime ... 58
meetings ... 22
midpoints ... 5, 57, 83, 84, 85
midyear issues ... 82
mindset ... 92, 140, 141, 143, 144
mission and vision statements ... 12
motivation ... 2, 92, 93, 116, 141
motivational games ... 88
multiple intelligences ... 90, 143
musical intelligence ... 91

N

National AfterSchool Association ... 2, 121, 141, 142
National Association of Elementary School Principals ... 2, 118, 119, 136, 142, 144
naturalist intelligence ... 91
negative behavior ... 26, 66, 96, 100, 103
negativity .. 2, 24, 30, 57, 75, 80, 82, 114
non-stop talker ... 98
non-verbal communication techniques ... 135
nutrition ... 12, 100, 101

O

office staff ... 48, 58
Ohio Association of Elementary School Administrators ... 2, 120
Ohio Classroom Management Project ... 15
old guard ... 35
orators ... 72

P

parental involvement ... 21
parents ... 2, 13, 15, 19, 20, 21, 26, 29, 30, 33, 35, 37, 43, 45, 49, 53, 57, 58, 59, 61, 66, 70, 71, 84, 91, 92, 94, 95, 108, 112, 113, 114, 115, 116, 120, 123, 124, 130, 133, 134
persistence (grit) ... 93
personal injury ... 48
personal notes ... 89
pictures ... 18, 34, 58, 59, 68, 70, 91, 100, 115
Plan, Do, Study, Act ... 26
planning ... 12, 22, 25, 26, 39, 41, 53, 58, 59, 62, 64, 79, 82, 83, 94, 98, 107, 112, 114, 119, 120, 123
planning time ... 50
play time ... 61
playground ... 3, 26, 27, 63, 64, 83
positive behaviors ... 1, 4, 6, 12, 19, 38, 52, 75, 80, 90, 113, 118
positive phone calls ... 89

power gaps 66
principal (school)........3, 80, 81, 119, 133, 134, 141, 144
procedures................................23, 44, 69
professional level performance 126
professionalism 80, 115
promotional events.............................118
proximity 18, 29
public relations 26, 30, 114
punishment 14, 15
Purple Cow 103, 105, 113

R

random acts of kindness.....................68
reading 1, 43, 81, 88
Reading Recovery 43
red card 59
regulatory agencies...............................71
relationships........17, 18, 19, 29, 63, 66, 94, 113, 118, 126, 127, 141, 144
reliability 93
resonation...19
respect.........18, 29, 30, 32, 42, 50, 119, 120, 128, 129, 133
responsibility checklist.............133, 134
restroom breaks 44
rigor..87

S

safety.......12, 19, 21, 27, 28, 30, 33, 38, 58, 70, 71, 96, 132
school buses..114
school officials......................................72
school-age children..............................66
school-based programs 26, 33
shared responsibility.................... 82, 133
sickness 48
site-director.....24, 43, 46, 48, 49, 65, 98
social media...................... 18, 21, 90, 103
social-emotional development............66
spatial intelligence 91
staff and student handbook 21
staff huddle.. 25
state and federal laws 22
stress 58, 96
structural analysis and assessment.....37, 38, 39, 53, 54, 55, 83, 84, 85, 97, 108, 109, 123, 124, 125, 126
structure...........1, 2, 3, 4, 6, 35, 39, 41, 46, 53, 58, 70, 72, 114, 127
substitutes 47
supervision 12, 26, 32, 37, 38, 42, 47, 57, 58, 60, 61, 62, 63, 64, 69, 79, 82, 98, 123
supervisory norms 44
supervisory plan...................... 37, 38, 83

T

That Kid... 68
time-on-task 48
tips and advice 121
Tortoise and the Hare 106
toxic stress 20
transitions 12, 26, 30, 57, 68
transportation personnel.................. 114
trauma..20, 96
triggers 68
trust.......................................30, 68, 129
twenty-minute meeting....................... 81

U

uniform policies.................................. 33

V

vocabulary... 71
volunteer(s).............21, 28, 50, 116, 120
vulnerability 19

W

website.................................... 16, 21, 30
West School... 2

Other Books by Paul G. Young

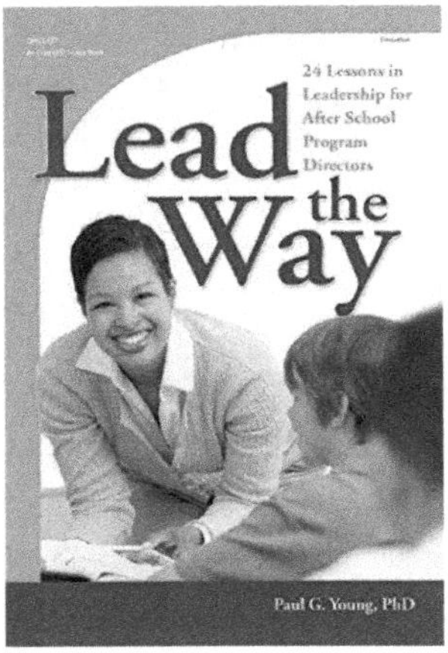

Lead the Way provides short, self-guided overviews of leadership topics that both aspiring and practicing afterschool professionals need to thrive in their roles. The 24 fundamental insights and strategies can be used as professional development topics with afterschool program staff, laying the foundation for the program to recruit, retain, and grown effective leaders. Highly popular content shared at National AfterSchool Association and state-affiliate conferences.

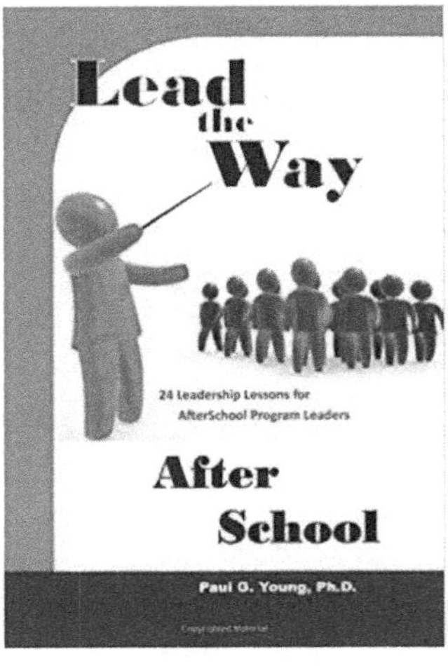

Lead the Way After School provides influential lessons that will help both aspiring and practicing afterschool professionals become knowledgeable and competent leaders. Readers are encouraged to include this book with ***Lead the Way*** (ExtendED Notes, 2014) in order to expand their awareness of important topics and challenges that afterschool professionals face. Included in this book are lessons pertaining to:

- Networking with Other Professionals
- Teaching Positive Classroom Management
- Instilling the Virtues of Grit and Growth Mindset
- The Power of Deliberate Practice
- Increasing Parent Involvement
- Improving Public Speaking
- Helping Students (and Adults) Become Better Listeners
- Dealing with Difficult Staff
- Reframing Issues
- Planning for Leadership Transitions
- and more...

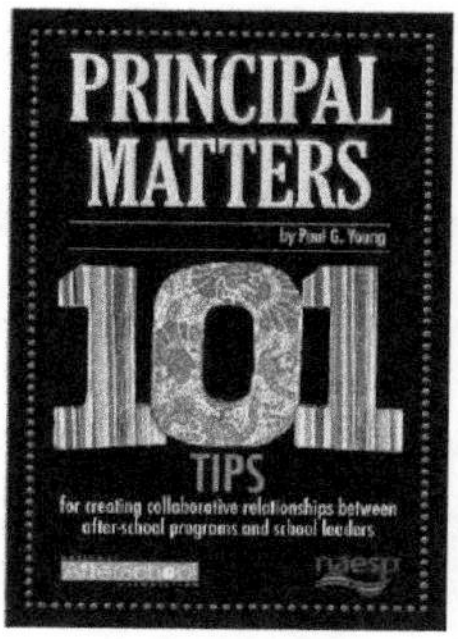

Despite the day-to-day accomplishments that every afterschool program director and staff member should enjoy, there often can be an equal number of challenges that afterschool professionals face. One strategy to clearing these daily hurdles is to build strong bridges between your afterschool program and the school principal. ***Principal Matters*** provides suggestions in ten areas, including tips that enhance student learning, tips that support principal/program director collaboration, tips that develop advocacy for afterschool programming and tips that support parent and community engagement. Whether you are new to the afterschool field or a veteran, these 101 tips provide positive ideas that will lead to quality programs and positive relationships between afterschool programs and school leaders.

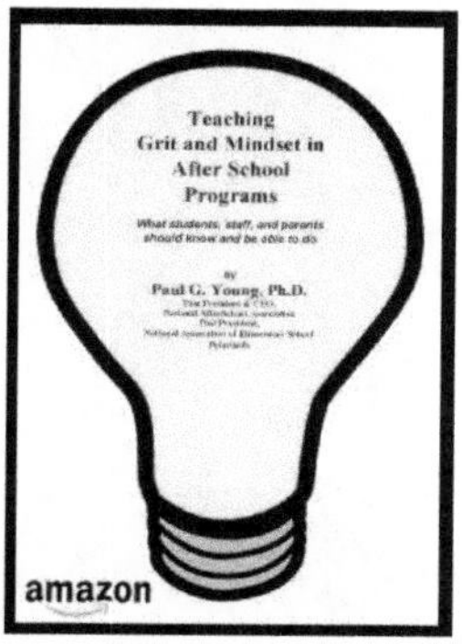

Teaching Grit and Mindset in After School Programs is an easy-to-use, hands-on guide for understanding and teaching the success skills – grit and mindset – in the afterschool program environment. Are you working with kids in your afterschool program who have potential but don't want to do anything? This is a commonsense resource for busy program leaders and their staffs who face the challenges of helping kids increase their perseverance and develop the mindset and motivation to complete homework and fully engage in out-of-school learning experiences. This book is packed full of ready-to-use professional development ideas, resources, trips, vignettes, and instructional activities. It is organized in four parts, five chapters with in each part.

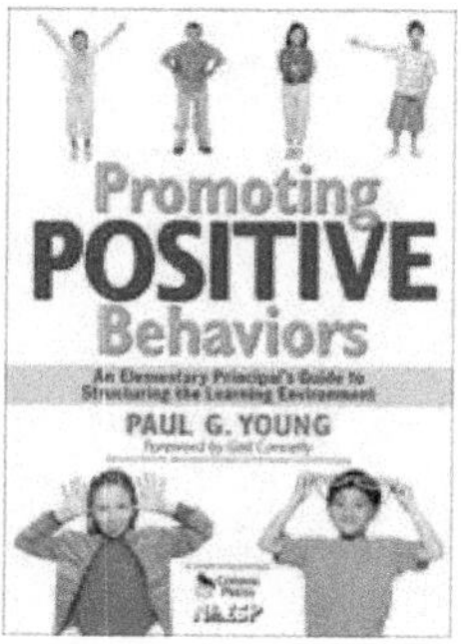

Promoting Positive Behaviors is an authoritative, commonsense resource for busy principals who face the challenges of establishing and implementing processes that promote positive student behavior and improve schoolwide performance. It offers valuable lessons and recommendations that affirm best practices, anticipate potential problems, and achieve a cohesive and cooperative teaching and learning environment. Readers will find procedures for everything from establishing a daily schedule and making announcements to monitoring behaviors for field trips and assemblies. This handbook is sure to be referenced again and again by aspiring, novice, and veteran administrators and is a companion to ***Promoting Positive Behaviors After School.***

ABOUT THE AUTHOR

Dr. Paul G. Young, Ph.D., has worked as a high school band director, elementary and junior high classroom teacher (grades 4, 5, and 7), nearly 20 years as an elementary school principal, and as an executive director of an afterschool program, all near the area of Lancaster, Ohio. For more than 45 years he has also served as an adjunct professor of music classes at the Ohio University-Lancaster campus. He holds a bachelor and master's degrees in music from the Ohio University School of Music. His doctorate, in Educational Administration, is from the Patton College of Education, Ohio University, Athens, Ohio.

He served in leadership roles with both the National Association of Elementary School Principals (NAESP) and the National AfterSchool Association (NAA). He was elected as president of the 30,000-member NAESP in 2002-2003. He served as a member of the NAA Board of Directors starting in 2008 before becoming NAA's President and CEO in 2010. He retired from association work in 2012. He has written extensively on the topic of school and afterschool alignment, led training workshops throughout the country, and played an influential role in the development of practical, evidence-based alignment strategies for school leaders and afterschool professionals. He is the author of several books for principals, music teachers, and afterschool professionals.

Dr. Young and his wife, Gertrude, a retired music teacher, live in Lancaster, Ohio. They have two adult daughters and sons-in-law. Katie and her husband Jon Steele live in Glendale, Wisconsin, where she is the principal oboist with the Milwaukee Symphony. She previously performed with the New World Symphony and the Florida Orchestra. Jon is the Field Marketing Director for the Eastern U.S. for Medshape, an Atlanta-based medical group. Mary Ellen and her husband Eric live in Glen Ellyn, Illinois. Mary Ellen is Senior Market Development Manager for McGraw Hill-Higher Education and Eric is a designer for Looney and Associates, Chicago.

Dr. and Mrs. Young enjoy their four grandchildren - Nora Rahn, Charles Steele, Evan Rahn, and Jonathan Paul "Jack" Steele and hope they each grow to enjoy a life filled with positive learning experiences – in school and after school.

References and Recommended Reading

Brafman, O. & Brafman, R. (2010). *Click: The Forces Behind How We Fully Engage with People, Work, and Everything We Do.* New York: Crown Publishing.

Breaux, A., & Wong, H. (2003). *New Teacher Induction: How to Train, Support, and Retain New Teachers.* Mountain View, CA: Harry K. Wong Publications.

Brinkman, R., & Kirschner, R. (2006). *Dealing with Difficult People: 24 Lessons for Bringing Out the Best in Everyone.* New York: McGraw-Hill.

Crenshaw, D. (2008). *The Myth of Multitasking: How Doing it All Gets Nothing Done.* San Francisco: Jossey-Bass.

Danker, Arndt, W., W., Bauer, W., & Gingrich, F. W. (2000). *A Greek-English lexicon of the New Testament and other early Christian literature (3rd ed).* Chicago: University of Chicago Press. p. 609.

Deasy, R. *editor.* (2002). Arts Education Partnership (2002). Critical Links: Learning in the Arts and Student Academic and Social Development. Washington, DC: Arts Education Partnership. https://www.aep-arts.org/

Dweck, C. (2006). *Mindset: The New Psychology of Success.* New York: Random House.

Di Giulio, R. (2007). *Positive Classroom Management: A Step-by-Step Guide to Helping Students Succeed (Volume 3).* Thousand Oaks, CA: Corwin Press.

Duckworth, A. (2016). *Grit: The Power of Passion and Perseverance.* New York: Scribner, Simon & Schuster.

Ericcson, A., & Pool, R. (2016). *Peak: Secrets from the New Science of Expertise.* New York: Houghton Mifflin Harcourt Publishing.

Fisher, D. & Frey, N. (2016). Two Times Ten Conversations. ASCD. September 2016, 74(*1*), pp. 84-85.

Gardner, H. (1983). *Frames of Mind: The Theory of Multiple Intelligences.* New York: Basic Books.

Godin, S. (2003). *Purple Cow: Transform Your Business by Being Remarkable.* New York: Portfolio/Penguin Group.

Gordon, J. (2007). *The Energy Bus: 10 Rules to Fuel Your Life, Work, and Team with Positive Energy.* Hoboken, NJ: John Wiley & Sons.

National AfterSchool Association. (2009). *Code of Ethics: NAA*. Oakton, VA. https://naaweb.org/images/NAA-Code-of-Ethics-for-AferSchool-Professionals.pdf

National AfterSchool Association. (2011). *Standards on Healthy Eating and Physical Activity (HEPA) in Out-of-School Time (OST)*. Oakton, VA. https://naaweb.org/resources/naa-hepa-standards

National Association of Elementary School Principals. (2005). *Leading After-School Communities: What Principals Should Know and Be Able to Do*. Alexandria, VA. NAESP (pp. 44-45).

Marzano, R. (2011). Relating to Students: It's What You Do That Counts. Educational Leadership, ASCD. Vol. 68, No. 6, pp. 82-83.

Maxwell, J. (2002). Leadership 101: *What Every Leader Needs to Know*. Nashville, TN: Thomas Nelson.

Payne, R. (1996). *A Framework for Understanding Poverty*. Highlands, TX: aha! Process, Inc.

Vollmer, J. (2010). *Schools Cannot Do It Alone: Building Public Support for American's Public Schools*. Fairfield, IA: Enlightenment Press.

Whitaker, T (2015). *Dealing with Difficult Teachers*. New York: Routledge/Eye on Education.

Young, P. (2014). *Lead the Way!: 24 Lessons in Leadership for After School Program Directors*. (Lewisville, NC: ExtendED Notes/Gryphon House.

Young, P. (2009). *Principal Matters: 101 Tips for Creating Collaborative Relationships Between After-School Programs and School Leaders*. Lewisville, NC: School Age Notes/Gryphon House.

Young, P. (2008). *Promoting Positive Behaviors: An Elementary Principal's Guide to Structuring the Learning Environment*. Thousand Oaks, CA: Corwin Press.

Young, P. (2018). *Teaching Grit and Mindset in Afterschool Programs: What Students, Staff, and Parents Should Know and be Able to Do*. Columbia, SC: CreateSpace.

Printed in the USA
CPSIA information can be obtained
at www.ICGtesting.com
LVHW012012111124
796318LV00002B/144
9781793141514